The Product-Safety Function: Organization and Operations

by E. Patrick McGuire

A Research Report from The Conference Board

About This Report

This report describes the organizational arrangements being made by U.S. manufacturers to ensure effective coordination of their efforts to produce safe products. It is based primarily on mail survey responses of about 300 manufacturing companies—all of them among the country's 2000 largest. In addition, supplementary information was obtained both by interview and correspondence from several other sources. These include product-safety specialists in selected retail firms; various safety authorities and consultants; representatives of trade associations and government agencies; and a number of manufacturing company executives attending product-safety seminars conducted by The Conference Board.

Contents

Tables

Exhibits

Foreword

ENLIGHTENED MANUFACTURERS have always taken prudent steps to assure the inherent safety of their products. But a variety of pressures in the 1970's have forced numerous companies to invest even more of their energies and resources in the formulation and maintenance of expanded product-safety programs

This added attention stems in part from recognition of the severe financial penalties that such burdens as product recalls and liability suits can directly impose upon a business. There is awareness, too, that the indirect costs of marketing unsafe products can be even more onerous. Nowadays, consumers, the media, and government agencies are acutely aware of safety miscues, which often are widely publicized. And the firm that trespasses the bounds of product safety does so at the possible risk of permanent market loss.

For such reasons, many managements have recently questioned whether their companies were organized as effectively as they might be to meet their necessary commitments to product safety. The results of this kind of soul-searching and organizational readjustment are examined in the present study. The investigation confirms that, until the early 1970's, relatively few firms maintained a separate, formal product-safety function. More often, safety responsibilities were assigned internally on an informal basis and were judged to be the implicit concern of those scattered units and individuals in the company who designed, produced and sold its products.

For some firms, such arrangements may still offer the most practical way to ensure product safety. But, opting for more formal approaches, many others have worked out alternative organizational answers in hopes of achieving better coordination of their product-safety activities. As this report reveals, some have established separate staff units for this purpose. Others have added the coordinating task to the other duties being performed by an existing function—such as occupational safety, quality assurance, and so on. In the multidivision firm, senior management has often reconsidered the appropriate nature and extent of product-safety assignments at corporate, group or division levels. Its decisions have usually taken into account the pace of safety activities being carried at each level, as well as the overall needs of the company.

At the same time, managements have sought to define safety-related issues more precisely throughout their companies. One aim sometimes is to make every employee more safety conscious, with the mission of ensuring safe products judged too important and too broad to be delegated to any single group of specialists.

The fact is that, even now, few companies have been entirely satisfied with the organization of their product-safety efforts or with the various procedures by which they attempt to monitor safety performance and respond to product-safety emergencies. This accounts for the flurry of experimentation still under way. For a candid reporting on how their own efforts in these areas are working out so far, The Conference Board is indebted to the hundreds of individuals and firms cooperating in this study. This report is a product of the Board's Marketing Management Research Department (Earl L. Bailey, Director), which is a unit of the Management Research Division (Harold Stieglitz, Vice President).

KENNETH A. RANDALL
President

Chapter 1

The Product-Safety Environment

DURING THE PAST DECADE, U.S. consumers have become increasingly concerned over, and aware of, the safety of the products and services they use. And this concern seems well-founded. According to the National Commission on Product Safety, accidents outside the workplace involving consumer products produce 20 million injuries each year. An estimated 110,000 of these injuries reportedly result in permanent disability, and 30,000 persons die each year in product-related accidents. In addition, workplace accidents from unsafe products take the lives of thousands more persons. And despite the enactment of safety statutes, and the creation of safety regulatory agencies, the toll continues to climb. Mounting pressures—economic, legislative, regulatory, social and political—have made manufacturers further aware of the critical importance of producing safe products.

This report examines how companies are making their organizations more responsive to product-safety issues. The primary focus is on those companies that have "formally" established product-safety functions—that is, those whose managements have taken special pains to assign product-safety responsibilities to departments, individuals or committees within their companies.

The safety organizational needs and possibilities of companies vary widely. For example, some products and services, by their very nature, seem to pose relatively little risk of injury to their users. Therefore, the absence of a formalized product-safety function within a company making or selling certain items is clearly no indication of callousness toward safety issues.

Although the major focus of this investigation is on practices relating to "consumer" products, this is not entirely the case. Some such products—tools and other light equipment—also find their way into the workplace environment where safety concerns are equally important and are perhaps monitored by the same units in the producing firms. In addition, the tasks of work-safety and product-safety managers are so intertwined in some companies that it is not always possible to completely separate them.

Behind Management's Concerns

Among the companies surveyed, four factors are cited most often as having been of primary importance in motivating managements to establish formal product-safety responsibilities—apart from the obvious moral and humane considerations involved. These are:

(1) Concern over existing and potential product-liability litigation.

(2) Concern over the potentially adverse effects of product-safety failures on the firm's reputation and sales, and the costs such failures entail.

(3) The need to comply with a variety of federal and state safety statutes.

(4) The need to monitor the potentials for safety risks in the company's product mix.

Soaring Product Liability

No one knows the total value of claims and suits filed against manufacturers for injuries relating to product use. There is evidence suggesting that hundreds of thousands of individuals are pressing claims for damages allegedly sustained as a result of unsafe or defective products. [1]

There are also data showing that the number of product-liability suits now in the courts has at least doubled—and some sources suggest that it may have quadrupled—during the past half decade. Obviously, the impact has been greater in some manufacturing sectors than in others. But the overall rise in actual or potential liability litigation has touched nearly every firm's operations and has been a leading factor in sensitizing companies to the matter of product safety.

Executives surveyed say that their companies' managements are worried especially about the frequently generous—sometimes staggering—awards to successful plaintiffs. An insurance industry consultant has calculated that the amount of money paid out in settlements—both in or out of court—rose 686 percent in the eight years between 1965 and 1973, increasing from an average of $11,644 to $79,340 per settlement. [2]

In many cases, claimants are said to be receiving awards which substantially outweigh the actual damages—that is, the economic damages—provable to the court. For example, a 1975 study of the 79 largest incidents of loss, conducted by the American Mutual Insurance Alliance, showed that, on average, the settlements made for injuries to injury victims and their survivors amounted to $9.02 in tax-free cash payments for every $1.00 of economic loss sustained up to the time of the settlement.

Moreover, the large sums reportedly awarded to successful plaintiffs represent only the *direct* payments to them. It is estimated by one legal group that the costs of defending a product-liability suit amount to about 30¢ per dollar of settlement claims paid. [3] The costs include attorney's fees, court costs, fees for expert witnesses, and so forth. But insurance industry sources say that the aggregate of "indirect" costs that companies incur as a result of product-liability litigation nearly always exceeds the amounts awarded to injured parties.

It is evident that even those companies that are not the direct target of product-liability suits pay a price for the current explosion in product-liability litigation. The toll is exacted through dramatic increases in the cost of product-liability insurance—insurance which most of them must have to protect against potentially calamitous losses or to qualify them as vendors to major retailers and distributors. It is also reflected in the difficulty that some firms face in even obtaining product-liability insurance at any cost.

While overall premiums paid for product-liability insurance increased 65 percent in a recent six-year period, a U.S. Department of

---

[1] Just how many product-liability suits are filed is also unknown. What is equally uncertain is how many claims for redress have been made and settled out of court. During its research, the Inter-Agency Task Force on Product Liability of the U.S. Department of Commerce was unable to pinpoint the exact number of lawsuits involving product liability. Estimates by various observers range from the 30,000 to 40,000 suits per year (suggested by plaintiff association groups) to as many as 1,000,000 (suggested by a few observers in the insurance industry). Jury Verdict Research, a legal reporting service serving attorneys, puts the figure at 200,000 suits per year.

[2] Robert Larsen, an independent insurance consultant, in data presented to the U.S. Senate Small Business Committee, September 7-9, 1976, Washington, D.C.

[3] According to data supplied by the Defense Research Institute, Madison, Wisconsin, an organization that represents the views of defendants (primarily business firms) involved in product-liability litigation.

Commerce study concluded that the premium increases in many sectors of business averaged more than 200 percent in three years.[4] According to testimony before a U.S. Senate hearing, some firms, primarily smaller producers, fear that the unavailability of product-liability insurance will eventually force them out of business.[5] (A few documented business failures, because of a lack of such insurance, have already taken place.)

Among the many companies concerned with the drain on resources imposed by soaring insurance premiums is the Koehring Company. An executive of the machine tool and construction equipment producer has explained: "For Koehring, product liability insurance premiums have jumped nearly 200 times what they were just 12 years ago . . . . It will take $30 million of our sales merely to earn a profit sufficient to pay the premiums for our product-liability and property-damage insurance. The result hits Koehring, its stockholders, and its employees right in the pocketbook."[6]

Other Costs of Product-Safety Failures

Managements report added worries over the other consequences—beyond those associated with product-liability claims—of possible miscues. Products that are incorrectly designed or manufactured, which must be recalled, cost their makers hundreds of millions of dollars each year. In a typical year, upwards of 25 million product units may need to be recalled.[7]

In recent years, all of the major auto producers have been involved in such recalls—several of these requiring the return of more than a million vehicles in each campaign.

Besides the direct costs incurred in recalling and replacing its products, a company must also bear the expense of the resulting losses in sales, damage to its reputation, and so on. These in turn can affect financing, personnel recruitment, and a host of other things vital to continuing corporate growth.[8]

An Abundance of Safety Statutes

Dozens of federal and state safety statutes were enacted during the past decade. Although U.S. industry has been subject to various safety regulations for many years—for example, the Pure Food and Drug Act of 1906 and the Federal Insecticide, Fungicide and Rodenticide Act of 1947—it was not until the 1960's that Congress moved actively into the regulation of work and product safety. The National Highway Traffic Safety Act (1966), the Coal Mine Health and Safety Act (1969), the Clean Air Amendments (1970), the Occupational Safety and Health Act (1970), and the Consumer Product Safety Act (1970) are but a few of the resulting statutes.

As product-safety laws have grown in number and complexity, companies have been forced to keep abreast of the implications for their operations, including the need in some cases to report regularly to government agencies on product-safety matters. Often, formal product safety units have been designed to manage this task. For most product-safety executives, regulatory record-keeping and reporting now constitute their principal duties (see Table 8).

More Complex Products

Their increasingly complex products have also been a factor in the desire of many manufacturers to formalize their product-safety

[4] The study, released in March, 1976, showed that certain sectors (such as machine tools, automotive parts and tires, transport equipment, chemicals, pharmaceuticals, toys, health equipment, sporting goods and firearms, paintings and coatings, plastics, motorcycles and general aviation manufacturing) were those more likely to incur product-liability lawsuits. Insurance association data confirm that some industries bear the heaviest burden in increased premiums for product-liability insurance.

[5] Testimony presented by the Small Business Service Bureau to the Small Business Subcommittee, U.S. Senate, September 7-9, 1976, Washington, D.C.

[6] Statement by Orville R. Mertz, then chairman and chief executive officer of the Koehring Company, in *Koehring News,* Autumn, 1975, p. 2.

[7] E. Patrick McGuire, ed., *Managing Product Recalls,* The Conference Board, Report No. 632, 1974.

[8] It is not unknown for the price of a company's stock to decline immediately following public announcement of the recall of one of its major products.

Exhibit 1: Product-Liability Checkpoints

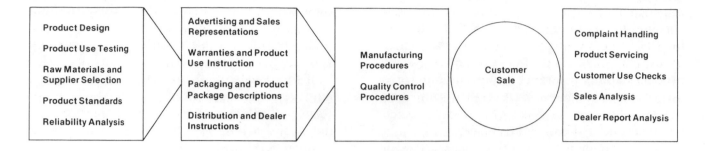

Product Design Product Use Testing Raw Materials and Supplier Selection Product Standards Reliability Analysis	Advertising and Sales Representations Warranties and Product Use Instruction Packaging and Product Package Descriptions Distribution and Dealer Instructions	Manufacturing Procedures Quality Control Procedures	Customer Sale	Complaint Handling Product Servicing Customer Use Checks Sales Analysis Dealer Report Analysis

Improving the company's product-safety record requires the institution of a series of both pre- and post-sale checkpoints. To begin with, the products' designers must be safety conscious and test their concepts of design and safety with customer-use tests. Reliable raw materials and suppliers must be specified and adequate product standards must be drafted. Marketers, for their part, must be certain that warranties and use instructions, as well as promises of product performance, do not invite misuse, and that responsible distribution channels are selected. Manufacturing must adhere rigidly to the established production and quality control procedures. And, after the product is in the customer's hands, satisfactory servicing procedures, effective complaint handling, along with customer usage analysis, can help reduce safety incidents and product-liability exposure.

responsibilities. As products become more complex, safety hazards tend to increase—sometimes, it is said, on an exponential scale. Predicting the nature and severity of risks posed by such products requires the attention of product-safety specialists. Recognition of the need for such expertise in a company has often been coincident with management's decision to establish a formal product-safety unit.

Safety executives interviewed cite numerous examples of the impact of product complexity on product safety. In the automotive sector there are nearly four times as many parts in today's autos as in those manufactured during the 1940's. New products in many industries have brought to the marketplace previously unknown and undetected hazards. For example, introducers of certain earlier models of color television sets were unaware that potential radiation hazards associated with the receiving tubes might require the need for a special shielding. Producers of some cookware items have had to contend with charges that their products failed to heat certain foods adequately enough to kill off harmful bacteria. The new offerings of several toy manufacturers proved dangerous to users because of unsuspected hazards.

Such incidents—or the possibility of them—have further stimulated the development of safety screening mechanisms of the kind often supplied by specialized product-safety personnel.

Patterns of Company Response

Although individual solutions to the problem vary, the companies surveyed have generally assigned product-safety tasks in one of four ways:

(1) *Ad hoc, one-time, issue-oriented responses.* A temporary task force, or perhaps a single staff specialist, is given a specific product-safety mission. This may pertain to a product recall, redesign of a product found to be unsafe, marshaling of defenses for a product-liability suit, meeting the requirements of a newly enacted safety statute, and so on. But the job has specific parameters—in both time and scope—so that the matter is "closed" once it is completed and there is no formal, ongoing effort.

(2) *Appointing a product-safety committee.* A product-safety committee, possibly bringing together the expertise of several different functions, may be charged with monitoring and overseeing certain product-safety activities. (Such committees do not necessarily enjoy sole jurisdiction over product safety, and they are often found in companies having full- or part-time product-safety specialists as well.)

(3) *Delegating safety responsibilities on a part-time basis.* The job of a designated executive, or perhaps a functional department, may be redefined or expanded to include product-safety.

(4) *Delegation of product-safety responsibilities on a full-time basis.* Product safety may be judged of sufficient importance to justify the full-time attention of a designated individual, group or unit in the company.

Origins of the Product-Safety Function

The origin of the safety function in a company often has a decided influence on its ultimate role and positioning. It is not unusual for the function to have begun—and, in some cases, to reside still—within one of the following areas: quality control, plant or work safety, insurance or risk management, legal, technical (research and development laboratories, engineering, etc.).

Most manufacturers have a formal quality-control function which monitors product standard, methods of manufacture, and so on. In many instances, the product-safety function had its beginnings there, with safety seen as a characteristic directly related to a product's quality (product-caused injuries arising from defects originating in the manufacturing process). And executives heading the separate product-safety units in a number of the companies studied began their careers as quality-control specialists.

A possible disadvantage that arises from such origins, product-safety executives point out, is that a firm's quality-control effort is likely to be internally oriented, and not actively attuned to customers' use of the product. Further, not all safety problems are the result of products being "defective" in a quality sense.

In other cases, safety began—and sometimes has remained—the traditional duty of safety engineers, individuals with primary experience in work safety and industrial hygiene. When these companies began to search for an executive or department to take on "product" safety responsibilities, they naturally turned to those having acknowledged expertise in the general field of safety.

Alternatively, a company's product-safety unit can sometimes be traced to an early emphasis on insurance-related expertise or issues. For example, as claims alleging injury from a company's products are processed, its risk-

Table 1: Age of Product-Safety Function

Age of Product-Safety Function	Nondivisionalized Companies	Divisionalized Companies		
		At Corporate Level	At Group Level	At Major Division Level
Less than 1 year	10%	16%	15%	9%
1 to 2 years	13	19	20	15
3 to 4 years	20	20	23	21
5 to 6 years	23	11	3	12
More than 6 years	33	34	39	44
Total	100%	100%	100%	100%

Note: Table refers to both full-time and part-time product-safety functions. Based on information provided by 30 non-divisionalized companies; and by 241 divisionalized companies, accounting for 130 product-safety units at the corporate level, 65 at a group level, and 115 at a major division level. Details do not always add to 100% because of rounding.

management or insurance specialists may come to play an active role in safety matters. Another reason such specialists may be asked to monitor product-safety matters is because the number and severity of injury claims has so direct a bearing on the costs and availability of insurance. In still other companies, product safety has occasionally taken on a legal cast.

Where the safety of a product is highly dependent on technical considerations, the primary orientation of the earliest product-safety personnel may have been research and development or engineering. Such personnel were perhaps assigned first to investigate and report on product failures, or to redesign products to minimize the dangers of injury.

There are many consumer products, of course, that are highly unlikely to cause major injury under any circumstances. A producer of such items in some cases may have elected, some time ago, to give product-safety jurisdiction to an existing department handling customer complaints—for example, the consumer affairs or customer relations departments. Later, safety specialists in these departments may have become heads of full-time product-safety units.

Table 2: Analysis of Survey Respondents by Products and Markets[1]

Products and Markets	All Companies	Divisionalized Companies[2]	Non-divisionalized Companies
Solely consumer	10%	7.1%	22.9%
Primarily consumer	22	22.2	22.9
Solely industrial	20	16.9	31.3
Primarily industrial	34	36.4	20.8
Consumer and Industrial	15	17.3	2.1
Total	100%	100%	100%

[1]Survey respondents include 251 divisionalized and 49 nondivisionalized companies.
[2]Details do not add to 100% because of rounding.

Behind the Rise in Product-Liability Litigation

While national safety statistics do not indicate significant change in the overall per capita product-injury rate, there has, nonetheless, been a measurable rise in product-liability litigation.

The American Mutual Insurance Alliance, an association representing the major product-liability insurance carriers, attributes this rise to several factors. Chief among these:

(1) Major changes have occurred in negligence law, principally with respect to the doctrine of strict tort liability, thus making it easier for consumers to sue manufacturers. In more than half of the states, it is necessary only to show that a product was "unreasonably dangerous"—not that the manufacturer was negligent—in order to succeed in a product-liability action.

(2) Public attitudes are said to have shifted toward a "psychology of entitlement." The underlying principle is that if an individual is injured, no matter who is at fault, someone—business, the community, the government—should be forced to pay for the injury.

(3) Consumer awareness and expectations regarding product performance and safety issues have grown substantially. Among the reasons why: national publicity associated with recalls of automobile and other products; discovery of harmful effects of various chemicals and drugs; and the activities of consumer groups and regulatory agencies.

(4) The U.S. system of legal compensation tends to encourage litigation. This nation is one of the few industrialized countries that allows attorneys to charge contingency fees and gain a large share of the rewards accruing from a successful product-liability suit.

Companies have attempted to counter the product-liability dilemma by lobbying the public to be more conscious of the fact that it is consumers—through higher prices for consumer goods—who are paying the cost of exorbitant product-liability awards. Insurance firms, trade association groups, and the like, have mounted publicity campaigns aimed at making this point. Sometimes, however, these efforts backfire. One major insurance company, for example, has been sued by a trial lawyers' association for unfair and deceptive advertising and for "jury tampering" in connection with its ads.[1]

[1]"Insurance firm is charged with deception in publicizing product liability problem," *Product Safety and Liability Reporter,* December 16, 1977, pp. 906-907.

Product Safety's Impact on Dealers and Distributors

In recent years, the plaintiffs in product-liability litigation have often included dealers and distributors as defendants in such litigation. While in most cases, should the plaintiff prove successful, the manufacturer picks up the tab for safety negligence, dealers nonetheless experience heavy costs in both time and legal expenses, regardless of their ultimate liability.

Nowhere has this situation been quite so evident or prominent as in the automotive sector. Here, customers injured by cars alleged to be safety defective often sue both the dealer and the automotive company. Such tactics have led the National Automotive Dealers Association to press car manufacturers to adopt an indemnification policy which would insulate the dealerships from liability costs—particularly the costs of legal defense—should the dealers be named as codefendants in product-liability actions. The major U.S. auto producers, and their foreign import competition, have responded to such pressures and have adopted dealer indemnification policies. These policies often take the form of a supplemental clause to the existing dealer sales and service agreement. The clause used by General Motors typifies the principal points covered in many auto dealer indemnification policies. General Motors agrees to protect its dealers against lawsuits arising out of: (1) a defect in the design, manufacture or assembly of the automobile; (2) claims that the automobile fails to meet promises or statements contained in General Motors' advertisements; (3) claims or suits resulting from product damages that existed prior to the time the product was delivered to the dealer—unless the dealer has been notified in advance about the damage prior to delivery of the product to the ultimate customer.

In return for these protections, the dealers agree that they will indemnify the auto manufacturer against all lawsuits based on a dealer's faulty repair, or a breach of sales contract with a customer, or as a result of false or misleading statements that they may make in their advertising or promotional efforts.

The president of General Motors, in explaining the reasons behind his company's desire to provide dealer indemnification, has said:

"With the recent increase in the number of product liability suits being filed, we [GM] have recognized that it has become more costly and time-consuming to defend them. Basically, General Motors has, in fact, assisted dealers where product liability suits made them parties to legal actions. Our announcement formalizes an indemnification clause as part of the dealer sales and service agreement and should relieve the dealer of many other problems relating to product liability litigation."[1]

[1]"GM, Ford launch indemnification plans," *Automotive News,* March 20, 1978, p. 1, 102.

The Impact of Product Safety and Liability on Small Business

The Select Committee on Small Business of the United States Senate in 1976 held hearings on the impact of product liability on small firms.[1] The hearings were prompted by numerous complaints directed to the Office of the President about the economic impact of sharply rising rates for product-liability insurance, as well as the inability of some firms to obtain such insurance. Among the evidence presented:

• A survey of 423 firms with fewer than 500 employees, conducted by the Small Business Service Bureau, found that product-liability premiums of over 21 percent of the firms had increased more than 100 percent over the previous two years; and 14 percent of the companies had been refused product-liability insurance in that period. Yet only 2.4 percent of these companies had ever had a product-liability claim registered against them. Three-quarters of the respondents favored establishment of an insurance pool which would make product-liability insurance available to any company that required it.

• Marsh & McLennan Inc., an insurance brokerage firm, reported: "Our experience indicates that rising costs and limited availability of product liability insurance is a severe problem for certain small businesses." It had found that "over the previous year increases of 300 percent (in premium costs) were not uncommon...and over a five-year period losses and loss adjustment expense have increased twice as fast as premiums."

• The general counsel for the Small Business Service Bureau cited findings by the Defense Research Institute that the average award in product-liability suits was now approaching $100,000, an amount he said was more than sufficient to bankrupt many small businesses. He stated: "The small business person is on trial in every product liability suit, even though he is not a party to a particular suit. Small manufacturers, for example, are defenseless in these suits, as they are often not parties to the litigation, yet they pay the cost in the form of increased product liability insurance premiums for each judgment and settlement."

• A study by the Iowa State legislature found that the total product-liability premiums paid by 128 small- to medium-sized companies rose in six years from $547,864 to $3,216,596—a six-fold increase. Premiums of some of the companies studied had increased 10 to 20 times.

• A spokesman for the National Small Business Association testified that self-insurance (called "going bare") is not a satisfactory remedy for the vast majority of all small businesses.[2] "Small business," he noted, "must rely on product liability insurance to cover the cost of legal actions. Even when declared not guilty, small firms do not have the resources of their larger competitors to cover their own legal costs. The threat of a lawsuit, in most cases, forces small firms to settle out of court, rather than take the chance of a jury awarding plaintiffs enormous judgments." He went on to say: "In many cases, insurance companies have canceled all product liability insurance for certain product lines. They do not distinguish between those manufacturers with good product safety records and those with bad records. Their feedback is too general to be useful to a particular industry."

• The National Association of Wholesaler-Distributors surveyed 400 of its wholesaler members and found that product-liability insurance premiums for 78.7 percent had recently increased. The median increase was 332 percent; and 53 percent of the respondents reported increases ranging from 100 percent to 1,000 percent. The general counsel for the association testified: "Although no correlation appears to exist between individual company premium increases and the company's litigation experience, preliminary review of the data does strongly suggest that rising litigation activity *within a product area* is reflected in general premium increases for wholesaler-distributors in that product area, irrespective of whether an individual company has experienced litigation."[3]

• The Recreational Vehicle Industry Association, representing over 500 manufacturers of recreational vehicles such as trailers and mobile homes, reported the results of a survey among its members: "Insurance rates have increased by anywhere from 200 percent or 300 percent.... in some cases to as much as 500 percent or 10,000 percent in the last few years. Some companies cannot find product liability insurance at any cost and a few have been forced to become self-insured.... *Although insurance premiums have soared incredibly, there has been no great increase either in the number of claims or in the amount of losses.* Other factors must be raising our insurance premiums such as insurance losses in other industries, investment losses by insurance companies and crude management decisions in underwriting departments. We have no information to indicate that product liability claims are especially common or unusually successful in the recreational vehicle industry. Our companies' premiums are no doubt being greatly affected by losses due to successful claims being made against other industries."

•A survey among the 31,000 manufacturing members of the National Federation of Independent Business found one small manufacturer in twelve reporting that it could no longer afford to carry product-liability insurance. Forty percent said they faced insurance renewal rate increases of over 100 percent.

[1]Hearings of U.S. Senate Select Committee on Small Business, Washington, D.C., September 8, 1976.

[2]Statement of Richard Tittle on behalf of the National Small Business Association, at the 1976 hearings.

[3]Statement of Harold T. Halfpenny, General Counsel, National Association of Wholesaler-Distributors, at the 1976 hearings.

The Impact of Fraudulent Insurance Claims

It has been estimated by one law enforcement officer that *one in every ten claims submitted to insurance companies is fraudulent* and that these claims cost the insurance industry approximately $1.5 billion per year.[1] Ultimately, of course, this cost is passed through to manufacturers, and then to consumers. It may also be a factor in some companies' assessment of their product-safety efforts. They believe—sometimes on more than an intuitive basis—that a certain number of the claims lodged against their products are, in fact, spurious. But the companies may have a difficult time convincing even the most sympathetic juries that these claims are not based in fact. The same law enforcement official has said:

"The most difficult problem facing a prosecutor presenting an insurance fraud case to a trier of fact is that most people just do not care about the [business] victim. It is not by chance that sophisticated con men and white-collar criminals do not steal from widows and orphans. The risk is greatly diminished when they steal from large, impersonal entities with 'deep pockets.' Thus, insurance companies, banks, or government agencies are perfect victims because many a trier of fact is not morally outraged by a theft from an organization against which he himself has felt victimized from time to time."

As noted, product-safety specialists acknowledge that the possibility of fraudulent claims makes their companies unusually wary. As the safety manager in a tool company reports: "We realize most claims are completely legitimate, but the occasional clinker we get does create an aura of suspicion, a kind of suspicion that has us looking at all claims two or three times."

[1]Robert J. O'Neill, "The Prosecutor and Insurance Fraud," *Legal Notes and Viewpoints.* New York, N.Y. The Practicing Law Institute, June 17, 1976, p. 1.

The Problem of Older Products

Often, safety executives must be concerned not only with today's products, but with those produced even decades ago which, by today's standards, may now be judged unsafe. This possibility creates difficulties for producers of durable equipment whose life extends over many years. For example, at the time of its manufacture a product may be completely safe in all respects, containing the necessary electrical grounding, mechanical safeguards, and so forth. But as the years pass, the equipment may become dangerous through misuse. It may even pass through the hands of several owners, each of whom may modify or perhaps abuse it. Nonetheless, if the equipment finally fails and a worker is injured, it is the original producer that is often the target of a product-liability suit.

In all of this, safety executives see a great deal of injustice. First, they point out that, though such a product may originally have met all the then-existing standards of safety, the manufacturer is in no position to force current users to maintain the machinery in a safe condition.

A survey by the National Machine Tool Builders Association found that one out of seven liability lawsuits against mechanical power press builders involved machines that were over 40 years old. In one out of four cases, the machine was over 30 years old; and, in almost half the cases, the machines were over 20 years old. A majority of the machines had been resold, modified and maintained at less than optimum levels of safety and technical proficiency.

It is ironic that a producer of exceptionally durable machinery—with exceptional life spans—is perhaps most vulnerable to such "elderly product" liability suits. One difficulty is that the statute of limitations in most states runs from the time that an accident occurs, not from the date of sale or delivery of the machine involved in it. Two cases illustrate the problems that this creates:

• A manufacturer sold a radial drill press to the General Electric Appliance Company in Chicago in 1937. The equipment was used throughout World War II for the production of military supplies and, after the war, was transferred to a GE plant in Rutland, Vermont. In 1969, 32 years after the delivery of the drill, an accident occurred in which a drill operator was injured. A suit filed for $150,000 against the drill manufacturer and the original distributor of the equipment was eventually settled out of court.

• In 1942 the Oliver Machinery Company sold a new bench saw to the United States Navy for use at Pearl Harbor. The machine was equipped at that time with the latest available safety equipment, including blade guards that differ only slightly from those now used by saw manufacturers. In October, 1971, a worker in an El Paso, Texas plant, which had bought the saw as surplus from the Navy, lost a part of his hand on this machine. The worker later testified that he was aware that the machine was dangerous and that the blade guard had been removed. The accident, according to the court testimony, took place when the worker attempted to cut a large piece of wood. The worker allegedly lifted the saw blade as he pushed the wood down the table, thereby pushing his hand through the saw blade and amputating his fingers. The machinery company argued that the accident could not have happened had the blade guard been installed—as it was on the original equipment when sold to the Navy 29 years earlier. Nevertheless, the jury found Oliver Machinery Company at fault and awarded the worker $50,000.

A few of the companies surveyed have attempted to mitigate potential damages of this kind by trying to persuade equipment users to make safety-related modifications, in some cases even supplying needed parts or guards at no cost.

In the long run, strict enforcement of state and federal work-safety regulations in all U.S. plants could alleviate such matters, several safety experts say. But they see little hope of that happening soon.

Chapter 2

Organizing the Product-Safety Function

THE KINDS OF PRODUCTS a company manufactures, its product-liability experiences, its basic organizational patterns, and a host of other factors influence the way in which its management organizes product-safety activities. No two companies studied have precisely the same organizational configurations for product safety.

The Options Available

One of the first questions management must decide is whether or not the company should have a "formal," full-time product-safety function. As noted earlier, some firms opt for temporary objectives, for what management regards as transient needs. Believing that they have only intermittent need for specialized product-safety help, others assign product-safety responsibilities on a part-time basis to persons having other duties as well. The alternative is to make product-safety the full-time responsibility of one or more major executives. The issue of whether product safety gets "full-time" or "part-time" attention does pose some important questions. For example, in very large organizations it is not unusual to find that the executive primarily responsible for product safety describes the responsibility as a "part-time one"—but that executive may be aided by a staff member who is fully occupied with product-safety responsibilities.

Corporate Organizational Structures of the Companies Surveyed

All 300 firms surveyed by The Conference Board are manufacturers (or have major manufacturing operations). Four out of five are divisionalized—that is, they are divided into two or more operating entities, each having production and sales capabilities. Most of the divisionalized companies also have group structures, with the executive heading each group overseeing two or more operating divisions. Here is the breakdown:

Total, all companies surveyed 300
Total, nondivisionalized companies
   surveyed 49
Total, divisionalized companies surveyed. . 251
  Divisionalized companies divided into
    multidivision groups 207
  Divisionalized companies without groups . 44

In addition, The Conference Board also contacted a number of major retailers who, because they often have major private-label product lines (or may even own manufacturing subsidiaries) are also vitally concerned with product-safety issues.

Table 3: Full-Time and Part-Time Product-Safety Functions in 266 Companies

	Companies Reporting	
Nature of Product-Safety Functions	Number	Percent
In nondivisionalized companies................................	48	100.0%
Full-time product-safety function............................	18	37.5
Part-time product-safety function	20	41.7
No formal product-safety function...........................	10	20.8
At corporate level in divisionalized companies...................	218	100.0
Full-time product-safety function............................	81	37.2
Part-time product-safety function	80	36.7
No formal product-safety function at this level	57	26.1
At group level in divisionalized companies[1]	144	100.0
Full-time product-safety function[1].........................	27	18.8
Part-time product-safety function[1].........................	56	38.9
No formal product-safety function at this level[1]............	61	42.4
At major division level in divisionalized companies.............	199	100.0
Full-time product-safety function............................	58	29.1
Part-time product-safety function	90	45.2
No formal product-safety function at this level	51	25.6
At lesser division level in divisionalized companies............	162	100.0
Full-time product-safety function............................	36	22.2
Part-time product-safety function	84	51.8
No formal product-safety function at this level	42	25.9

[1]207 of the 218 divisionalized firms that reported on this level of safety-function organization are organized into operating "groups."

Note: Based on information provided by 48 nondivisionalized and 218 divisionalized firms. Thirty-four firms surveyed (one nondivisionalized and 33 divisionalized) provided no specific information on this point. Percentage details do not always add exactly to totals because of rounding.

Choice of Organizational Levels

In nondivisionalized companies, product-safety assignments are, by definition, centralized if located at the firms' headquarters (see Exhibits 2 and 3.) (Occasionally, however, such assignments are delegated to outlying units, particularly production facilities in a kind of decentralized configuration—that is, there is no one present at company headquarters to assume such responsibilities or coordinate product-safety activities.)

In divisionalized companies, product-safety units may be found at a corporate level, a group level, a division level, or at several of these levels simultaneously (see Exhibit 4). Companies that have such a function only at the corporate level may be described as being fully centralized with respect to their product-safety organization. Those that have no function whatever at the corporate level, but have one or more functions at either a group or division level, may be considered decentralized.

But the vast majority of companies have elected to use a mixed organizational configuration, establishing full- or part-time product-safety assignments at both corporate and other levels (see Table 3). In relatively few of the firms studied is there an absolutely "pure" centralized or decentralized organizational design. The descriptions that follow are based on information from firms that have characterized their organizational arrangements as located *primarily* at a corporate, group or division level.

Corporate-Level Product-Safety Functions

Among those firms where product-safety responsibilities are primarily at a corporate level, the safety units are often relatively small and mainly perform a staff coordinating and consulting function. In a little more than one-third of the cases studied this unit operates on a full-time basis; in the other two-thirds product safety is a part-time assignment for the corporate-level executive in this activity.

In a quarter of the divisionalized companies, and one-fifth of the nondivisionalized firms, there is no "formal" product-safety function at corporate headquarters. That is, there is no one else who has product-safety duties described in his or her job specifications. This does not mean, however, that product-safety activities are never carried on at this level. In some instances, product-safety duties may be performed at irregular intervals on an ad hoc basis, and companies thus choose to describe the arrangement as "informal."

Divisionalized companies with only a corporate-level product-safety function most frequently report that their organization design choice was mainly influenced by one or more of the following:

(1) Product-safety issues in the firm are so sensitive or complicated that management does not wish to assign these responsibilities to lower organizational levels.

(2) Informal product-safety ac\ carried out at a group or division l\ formal function is required at \ headquarters in order to coordinate tivities.

(3) The company's organizational \ favors the placement of strong, specializ\ groups, such as those required to meet p\ du\ safety responsibilities, at a corporate leve\

(4) The company's groups or division\ \.\. the necessary experience and skills to mar\ \ 'e ' sophisticated product-safety program.

In general, the survey data show \ manufacturers of consumer goods are m\ likely to have full-time product-saf\ executives based at a corporate headquart\ level than are producers of industrial good\ . The newer the product-safety function—the more recently it was established—the more likely it is to exist primarily at a corporate level.

Group-Level Product-Safety Functions

As Table 3 shows, the majority of companies with divisions have established a group organizational structure—combining divisions with like products or markets. However, the existence of a formal product-safety function at the group level is relatively rare. Fewer than two in ten companies having group structures have a formal product-safety function at that level.

An analysis of those firms with group-level safety units shows that such a unit is most likely to be found in situations where:

(1) There is already a substantial collection of other staff resources—for example, legal, marketing, quality assurance—at that level.

(2) The divisions within each group are of modest size and have similar products, markets and product-safety concerns.

(3) Numerous divisions within a group may have part-time product-safety units that require coordination and monitoring by group-level staff function. As noted previously, it is relatively rare that a company has a "pure" organizational configuration as far as product-safety staffing is concerned—that is, the unit or

responsibility exists *only* at one level. This situation is especially true with regard to group-level product-level assignments. The majority of companies studied that have formal group-level assignments also have safety responsibilities, on either a full- or part-time basis, within one or more of the divisions in the several groups the company may have established.

As an example, one hand tool manufacturer has combined five of the firm's divisions into a power tool group. At the group level a vice president for product quality, who in turn has a director of reliability and safety assurance reporting to him, is the executive primarily responsible for the company's overall safety functions. In each of the group's five divisions, there is also a director of quality assurance who has a dotted-line relationship to the group vice president for product quality. In addition, the company has established a product-safety committee at the group level, comprised of representatives from engineering, quality control, legal, insurance, manufacturing and marketing.

The existence of group-level product-safety committees is an exception rather than the rule. In most firms, there would not be sufficient staff specialists at a group level to compose such a committee.

Divison-Level Product-Safety Functions

A minority of firms have chosen to completely decentralize the product-safety function, delegating the responsibility to each of the relevant divisions (not all divisions may have product-safety concerns or explosures). In a typical situation, a firm may have a product line consisting primarily of industrial goods, but it may also have one or two divisions producing for the consumer market. Such a company may have established product-safety units within the consumer goods divisions, but there are no corresponding functions in the industrial goods divisions, or at corporate headquarters. (Nevertheless, industrial divisions may have occupational-safety specialists, who could also be involved with product-safety matters.) In the case of several conglomerates studied, there is little corporate-level staffing, nor is there group-level support, and the job of product safety, as it is for most other responsibilities, is located at the operating level. An organizational configuration placing product safety primarily at the division level is often justified on these accounts:

(1) A company's product-liability risks, because of the nature of its products, may be concentrated in only the one or two divisions deemed "closest to the problem" and thus believed by management best able to handle their own safety requirements.

(2) A firm may have grown rapidly, primarily through acquisitions, and each of these acquisitions, which later becomes an operating division, may have had fully organized product-safety units. The parent firm may see little need to disband such units and may not have established a coordinating function at a group or corporate level.

(3) The products and services of each division may be so specialized and technical that the safety aspects of the products or services are best monitored and controlled at the division level.

(4) As a matter of overall company policy, divisions may be fully responsible for almost every aspect of their operations, with very little corporate- or group-level assistance.

(5) The operating divisions in some firms are of such gigantic size that it is improbable that a safety unit located at either a corporate or group level could provide much assistance to these super divisions.

It should be remembered that the fact that a company positions its product-safety responsibilities primarily at a division level does not mean that no members of the corporate staff are in any way involved in product-safety matters. The legal department, for example, is often an active partner in safety deliberations and is almost always located at the headquarters level. And in instances where companywide action may prove necessary, as in the case of product recalls, such functions as corporate-level advertising and public relations may also play an active role.

Mixed Corporate, Group or Division Product-Safety Functions

By far the largest number of companies studied favor a combined approach which brings together product-safety functions at both division (or group) levels with those at a corporate level. One of the most frequent arrangements is to establish a full-time function at headquarters with part-time safety assignments at operating levels.

In many instances, not all divisions of a company have product-safety units. It is not unusual, for example, to find a full-time safety executive at company headquarters working closely with part-time specialists in several divisions, while a few other divisions may have either a full-time safety assignment or no provisions for product-safety responsibilities at all. (The number of organizational permutations companies can employ, using the mixed responsibility approach, seems limited only by the number of divisions, groups, product lines, and so forth.)

As a general rule, companies prefer to establish full-time product-safety responsibility for the company as a whole, and within any division (or group) in which safety issues are of serious concern. Otherwise, as might be expected, division-level responsibilities are more apt to be handled on a part-time basis, with such assignments given to personnel in quality assurance, engineering, or research and development departments. Thus, most division-level product-safety work is part-time.

The Matter of Informal Product-Safety Assignments

Firms may choose to establish a formal product-safety assignment on either a full- or part-time basis. But companies may also decide to handle product-safety issues on an "informal" basis. By this it is meant that managements may be genuinely concerned about product safety, but may believe that safety responsibilities have been so fully integrated into the work assignments of the legal, consumer affairs, marketing, engineering or other departments that they are not regarded as separate functions—even if performed on a "part-time" basis. In other words, it is implicit in various executives' responsibilities that they

Exhibit 2: Example of Organizational Structure: Full-Time Product-Safety Function in Non-divisionalized Company

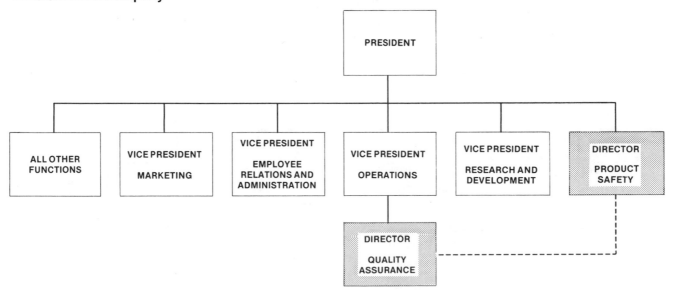

Exhibit 3: Examples of Part-Time Product-Safety Assignments in Nondivisionalized Companies

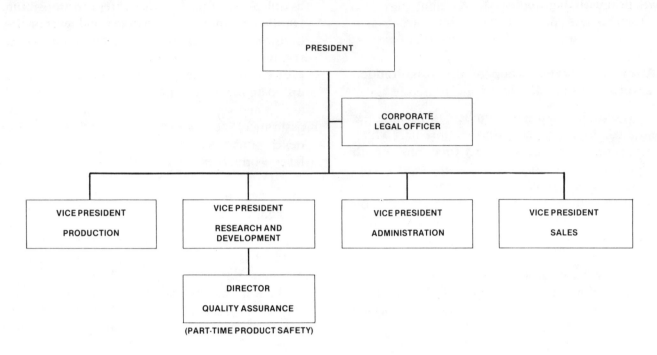

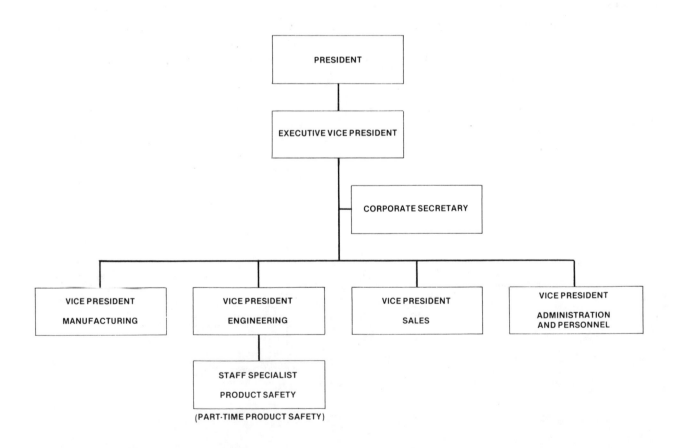

will take safety issues into consideration and will deal with them as they arise.

Companies taking such an approach often choose to characterize their delegation of safety responsibilities as "informal." Of course, an obvious question is who, in such instances, is most likely to handle significant product-safety matters when, and if, they arise. The answer, according to most of those reporting, is the quality-assurance unit at a divisional level or the occupational-safety unit at the corporate level. In a few firms, it is the head of engineering or research and development who assumes such responsibilitity.

Exhibit 4: Example of Organizational Structure: Divisionalized Company Having Full- and Part-Time Product-Safety Functions

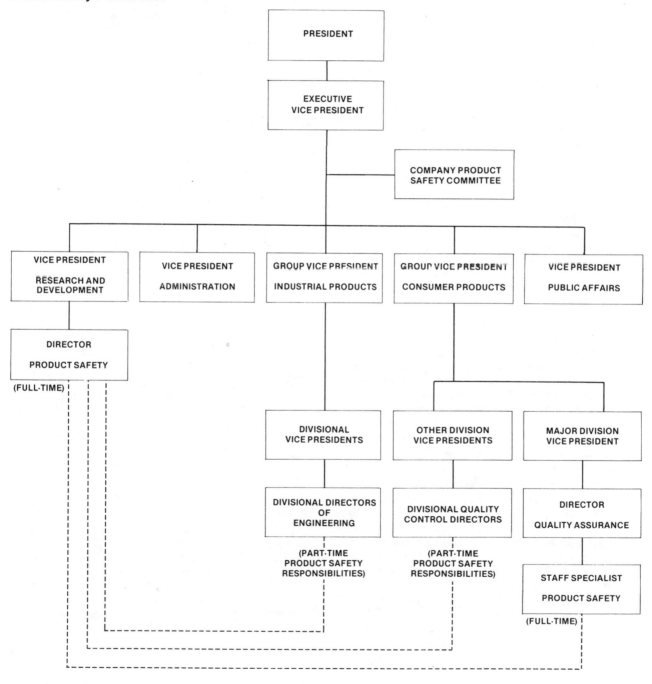

How Companies Position Product-Safety Responsibilities

The task of product safety, as described earlier, varies greatly among companies according to the kinds of products manufactured, the markets served, and by organizational philosophy. The following company experiences illustrate such variances.

Zenith Radio Company. At Zenith (see Exhibit 5) safety responsibilities are vested in the director of product compliance and evaluation. This executive, who reports to the senior vice president in charge of engineering and picture tube operations has substantial autonomy as far as safety matters are concerned. There are specialists on the safety-unit staff who deal with the engineering and design aspects of Zenith products, as well as their conformance to state and federal safety standards.

Compliance with manufacturing specifications, the testing of raw materials and components, and other routine quality-control matters are the tasks of a quality-control unit within the manufacturing group. However, there is a safety specialist on this quality-control staff who provides on-the-spot consultation on safety issues and reports, on a "dotted-line basis" to the corporate quality, reliability and safety engineering group.

Ex-Cell-O Corporation. Ex-Cell-O's work force of 11,000 plus employees is organized into seven operating groups. Each combines several subunits or divisions, some of which have a part-time product-safety assignment within their engineering or quality assurance departments. Overall responsibility for product safety is located at the corporate level, where it is combined with the legal and insurance functions in the corporate secretary's office (see Exhibit 6).

Bell & Howell Company. The corporate-level product-safety function at Bell & Howell is primarily filled by a committee whose members include the corporate director of quality assurance, as well as the general managers of the company's divisions. This safety committee considers a variety of companywide safety issues and reports through the corporate legal department to an executive vice president (see Exhibit 7).

Colt Industries Inc. Colt's management has decided that primary responsibility for assuring the safety of Colt products should rest within each operating division. But this decentralized configuration is reinforced by a corporate-level safety function to keep key division employees informed on safety matters. The headquarters unit is part of the risk-management office, headed by the director-risk management, who in turn reports to Colt's senior vice president of administration (see Exhibit 8).

Aluminum Company of America. A full-time product-safety manager at Alcoa's corporate headquarters reports to the vice president of corporate marketing. The corporate safety function gets substantial help from the company's legal and insurance staffs, also located at corporate headquarters, as well as from the directors of quality assurance working in various operating divisions.

Eastman Kodak Company. The corporate director of health, safety and security has the general responsibility for regulatory liaison and operating recommendations covering both product safety and occupational safety. Reporting to him, with specific concerns in regard to health and safety, are the corporate safety director, the director of the health, safety and human factors laboratory, and the corporate medical director. These corporate functions are supportive of each of the several divisions of the company which are engaged in manufacturing, marketing and distribution; ultimate responsibility for providing safe and healthful workplaces and safe products resides with line management. The corporate offices provide guidance, advice, certain testing and monitoring functions, and assistance in formulating policy and ensuring conformity to various laws and regulations regarding health and safety. Each manufacturing division also has quality control departments which provide line management with assurance that products not only meet the needs of the customer but are safe to manufacture and safe to use.

Retailing Firms. Although, as noted, this report—and its key exhibits and tables—deals primarily with the practices of manufacturing firms, information concerning their product-safety functions has also been obtained from various retailing organizations. Among major retailers, such as J.C. Penney and Sears Roebuck, product-safety responsibilities tend to be centralized. Often, the product-safety unit reports to a vice president of merchandising. At J.C. Penney, the product-safety manager, who reports to a product-service manager, chairs the fact-finding groups and participates in the corporate level safety-committee which is chaired by the vice

president of merchandise operations, and whose members include staff executives of consumer affairs, public relations, and merchandise services.

As might be expected, the role of product safety in retailing organizations varies somewhat from the manufacturing sector. Retailers are primarily concerned with evaluating products already in production—rather than with new product prototypes. But the fact that so many major retailers have an extensive private-brand product mix (for which they have primary product-safety responsibility) means that they are required to develop substantial expertise in the area of product safety. It is not unusual, in addition to the formal product-safety structures noted above, to find that large retailers also have one or two specialists in their legal departments who focus nearly entirely on safety issues—litigation, regulation and so forth.

Table 4: Functional Department Heads to Whom Product-Safety Matters Are Most Often Assigned, in Absence of Formal Product-Safety Function (Rank Order of Mention)

In Nondivisionalized Companies	In Divisionalized Companies			
	At Corporate Level	At Group Level	At Major Level Division	At Lesser Division Level
Title	Title	Title	Title	Title
Quality Assurance	Occupational Safety	Quality Assurance	Quality Assurance	Quality Assurance
Engineering	Quality Assurance	Administration	Engineering	Occupational Safety
Marketing	Insurance	Occupational Safety	Occupational Safety	Engineering
Occupational Safety	Research and Development	Engineering	Research and Development	(Not Listed)
(Not Listed)	Legal	(Not listed)	(Not Listed)	(Not Listed)

Exhibit 5: Product-Safety Organization—Zenith Radio Corporation

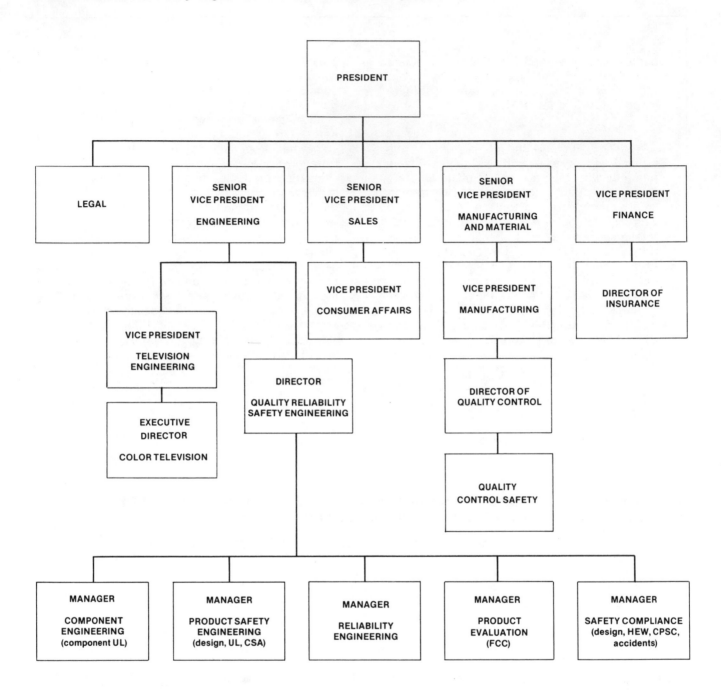

Exhibit 6: Product-Safety Organization—Ex-Cell-O Corporation

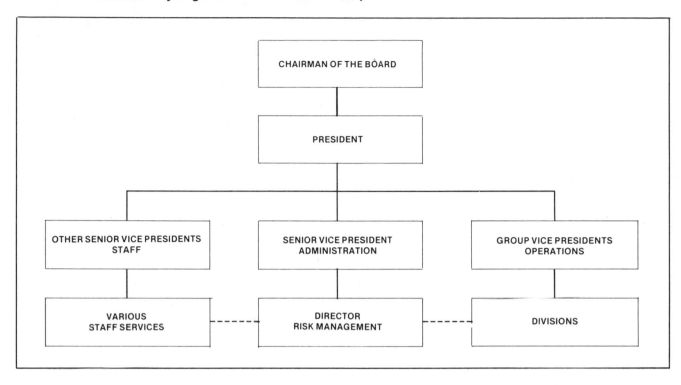

Exhibit 7: Product-Safety Organization—Bell & Howell Company

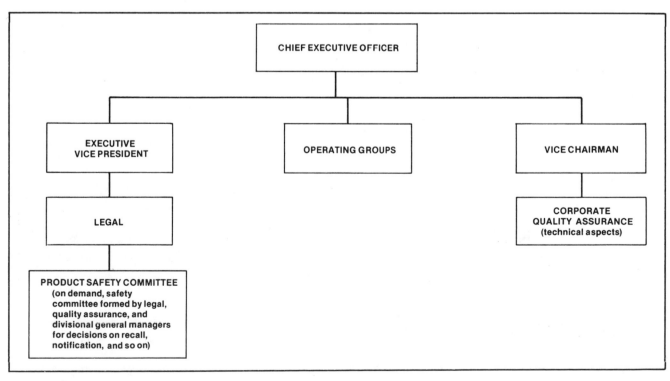

Exhibit 8: Product-Safety Organization—Colt Industries Inc.

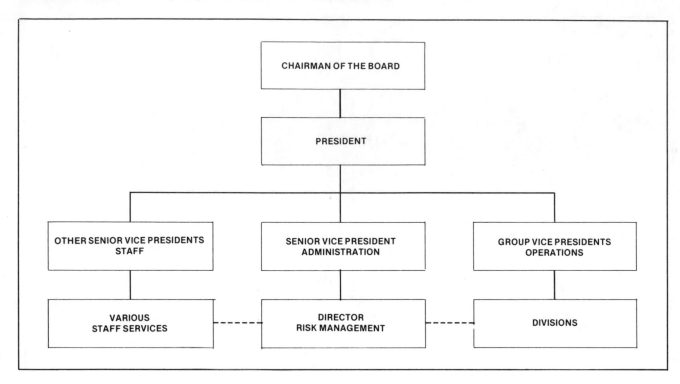

Exhibit 9: Product-Safety Organization—A Metals Manufacturer

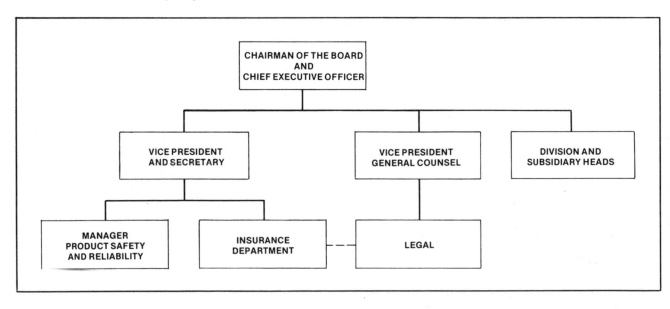

Exhibit 10: Product-Safety Organization—Eastman Kodak Company

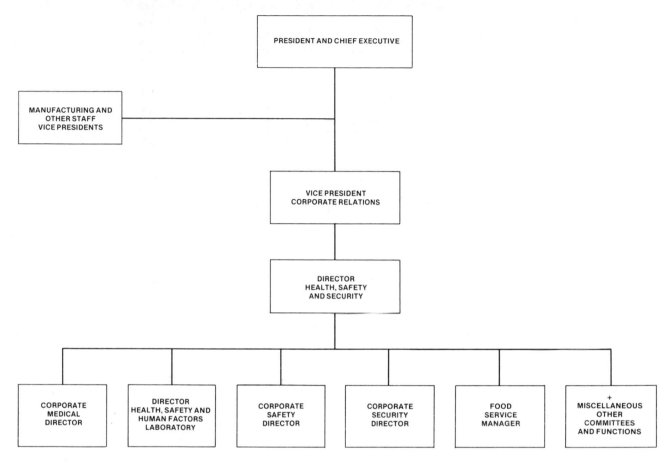

Exhibit 11: Product-Safety Organization—J.C. Penney Company

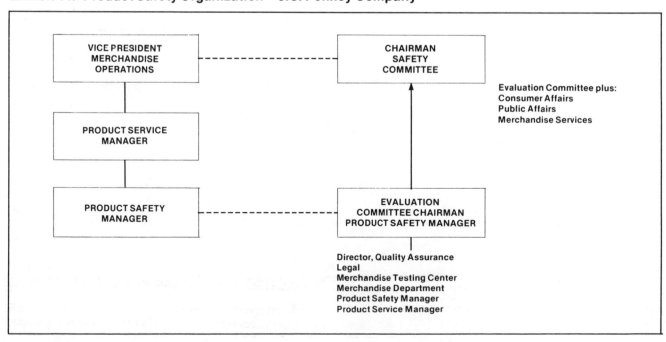

Exhibit 12: Corporate and Divisional Product-Safety Organization—Brunswick Corporation

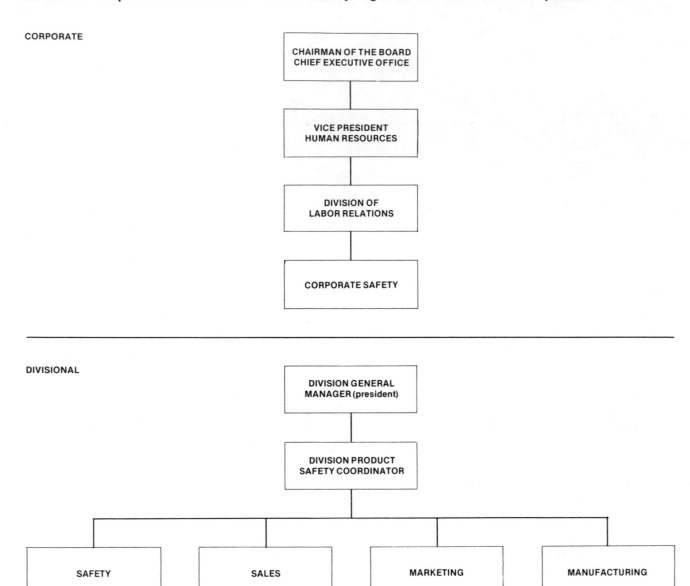

Exhibit 13: Corporate Consumer Affairs and Medical Products Division Quality Assurance Organization—3M Company

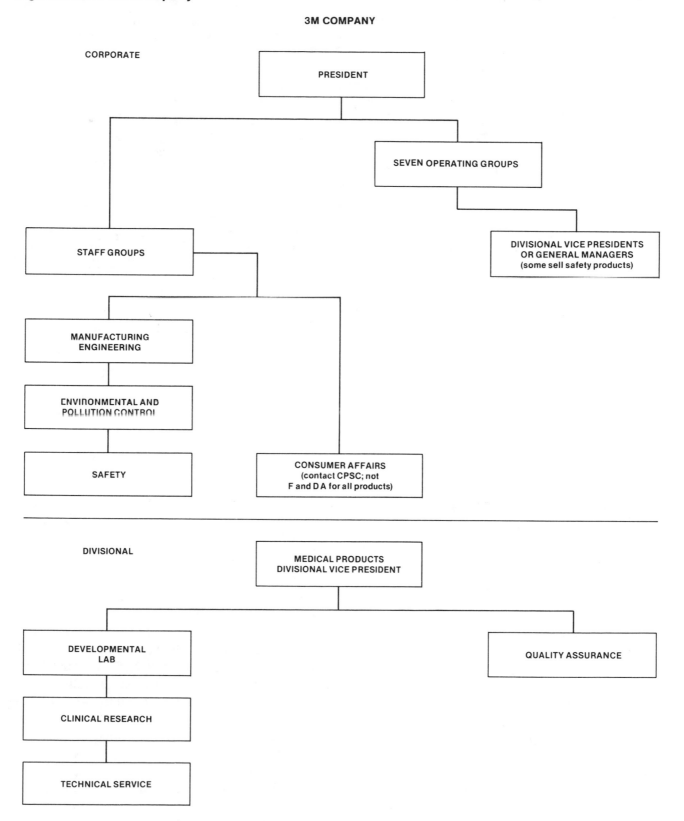

3M COMPANY

CORPORATE

PRESIDENT

SEVEN OPERATING GROUPS

STAFF GROUPS

DIVISIONAL VICE PRESIDENTS
OR GENERAL MANAGERS
(some sell safety products)

MANUFACTURING
ENGINEERING

ENVIRONMENTAL AND
POLLUTION CONTROL

SAFETY

CONSUMER AFFAIRS
(contact CPSC; not
F and D A for all products)

DIVISIONAL

MEDICAL PRODUCTS
DIVISIONAL VICE PRESIDENT

DEVELOPMENTAL
LAB

QUALITY ASSURANCE

CLINICAL RESEARCH

TECHNICAL SERVICE

Exhibit 14: Product Quality and Safety Organization, U.S. Power Tool Group—Black & Decker Manufacturing Company

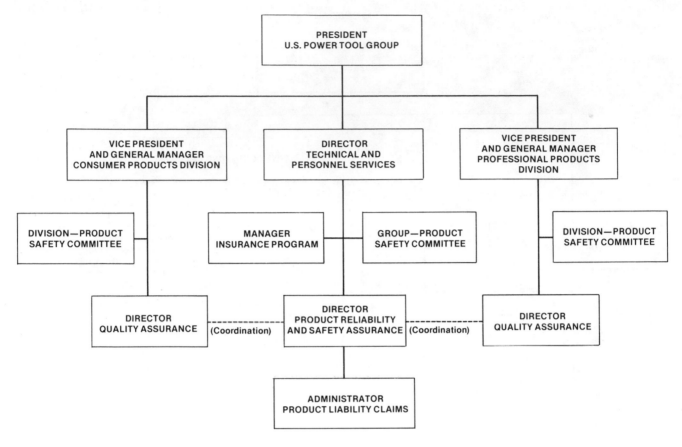

Factors Influencing Internal Organizational Variation

Even within companies, up to a third of the firms studied report that there is notable variation between their operating units, as far as product-safety organizational configurations and responsibilities.

Product safety executives cite four principal factors as those most likely to contribute to organizational variation. These are:

(1) The nature of the customer/users of the product.

(2) The degree of potential hazard present in the use of the products.

(3) The relative size of the company, division or operating unit producing the product.

(4) The specific safety laws and regulations to which producers of the products are subject.

Nature of Product's Users

The users of a product can be important in determining the type of product-safety functions that are selected. Obvious differences sometimes exist between different categories of users—such as individual consumers, industrial, institutional, professional, and so forth. There are differences that may exist as well between more frequent and less regular users of the products. In addition, customers for one product may be more sophisticated in using that product than are those of other products.

For a particular unit of a company, the possibility for product failures or misuse may be greater than for other company units. And greater liability risks may contain implications for product-safety organization. The vice president for the toy products division of one diversified manufacturing firm, in describing its approach to safety organization, states:

"Nearly all of our division's customers are preadolescents. We have to be extra careful in how we design our products, and communicate to both child and parent information about a product's proper use, and then be able to handle the claims in litigation that seem to be an inevitable part of this business. All of this requires a larger, and more complex divisional product-safety organization than we might otherwise need. But we can't afford the risk of anything less."

At times, a firm may not think far enough ahead to consider the "unusual" ways in which their products might be misused. In such instances, what are, at first glance, reasonable and complete precautions later turn out to be less than adequate.

For example, a division of a metals company, produces corrosive and potentially hazardous finishing solutions for metals fabricators. The company took some care to design a warning label which described, in copious text, the hazards of using these materials. The labels were affixed to drums of the product. But a major product-liability suit arose because an illiterate worker failed to heed such advice because he was simply unable to read the labels. The absence of any symbols, such as a skull and crossbones, failed to alert the worker to the fact that the label was describing hazardous conditions. There are a sufficient number of illiterate workers, product-liability attorneys point out, that companies should seriously consider the routine use of nonverbal symbols to alert them to product hazards.

In other instances, the product-safety organization may be influenced by the geographic locations or concentrations of customers. The producer of a medical device, for example, explains that nearly half its production is shipped overseas. Since safety specialists for the product must be near the site of injury or misuse, the firm has stationed such specialists in several of its overseas offices.

A product's distribution pattern is still another factor that sometimes influences safety organization. If products are sold through several layers of agents, distributors or wholesalers, for example, this may require a different kind of product-safety unit than if products are sold directly to their users. For example, one home appliance manufacturer, which markets its products directly to franchised dealers and which enjoys considerable control over this distribution channel, maintains only a small, relatively compact, product-safety group. Another firm, a competitor, which employs several distribution channels, has a much larger, more specialized product-safety organization. The latter company's contacts with various distributors and wholesalers during the course of product recalls, seminars on product use, and the like accounts for this difference.

Degree of Hazard

Because of their design, the ways or situations in which they are likely to be used, or like factors, some products inherently pose greater physical risks to their users than do others. Since the advent of the National Electronic Injury Surveillance System, a government monitoring system which daily tabulates the number and variety of product-related injuries consumers report to medical authorities, it is reportedly easier to judge these relative risks.

Not surprisingly, the most elaborate product-safety organizations are generally maintained by manufacturers of products that tend to produce a greater number of injuries—and are thus most likely to generate product-liability claims or litigation. The same observation is true for an operating division within a multidivisional firm. The nature of some divisions' products and their uses, poses greater safety risks than does others. In one company, for example, the product-safety function is generally the part-time responsibility of the quality assurance department in each operating division. An exception is a division that produces recreational products, a product category with a proven potential for serious injury. Within this division, product safety gets full-time attention, and the executive heading the function reports directly to the division's vice president.

It should be recognized that it is *the potential* for product injury that is often an overriding factor in product-safety organization. Such is the case in a division of an industrial company that produces flammable gases. While no major injuries have thus far occurred as the result of accidents involving use or misuse of products sold by the division, the risk potential is judged to be so great as to justify a safety structure for the division far more elaborate than that required of other divisions producing materials with less hazard potential. As the corporate product-safety director explains: "You can't wait until an accident or injury occurs to create a safety responsibility. We know that our products are inherently dangerous. Thus far, through luck or whatever means, we have been successful in avoiding injury. But the hazard is great and we need full-time safety professionals in order to maintain our safety record."

Size of Operations

There appears to be some modest correlation between the size of an operating unit and the size and scope of its formal product-safety assignments. Several safety executives say that some of the smaller divisions in their companies simply do not have staff budgets that permit the employment of full-time safety specialists. (In very few cases studied are full-time product-safety functions maintained in companies, divisions or operating units with gross sales volumes below $10 million.)

Impact of Safety Statutes

Safety executives report, that to some extent, the type and variety of safety laws to which their companies are subject does influence the organization of the firm's safety functions. A majority of executives surveyed indicate primary concern with federal safety regulations, even though faced with an increasing number of state and local safety statutes.

Table 5 summarizes the rank-order impact of various federal product-safety laws on the companies surveyed. When safety executives refer to the "impact" of various statutes, they are usually reporting on the amount of recordkeeping the law requires, the need to keep posted on regulatory changes to make certain their company's policies and procedures meet the legal requirements of the laws, as well as the civil and criminal impact that trespass of the law might occasion.

Obviously, firms making products subject to stringent safety laws are more apt to require more elaborate, formal product-safety functions than are other companies. In particular, as Table 5 illustrates, the Occupational Safety and Health Act (OSHA) is of major concern among all respondents—both from the standpoint of workplace standards and product standards. This is partly a reflection of the fact that a number of the company's safety units may have

Table 5: Federal Product-Safety and Related Statutes Pertaining to Products of 216 Manufacturers

---

Safety Statutes Affecting Company Products[1]

OSHA-Workplace Standards
Environmental Protection Act
Consumer Product Safety Act
OSHA-Product Standards
Hazardous Substances Act
Food Drug and Cosmetic Act
National Traffic and Motor Vehicle Safety Act
Flammable Fabrics Act
Radiation Control and Safety Act
Poison Prevention Packaging Act
Toy Safety and Child Protection Act
Boat Safety Act
Firearms Act
Refrigerator Safety Act

[1]Listed in order of frequency of mention as directly affecting products of a company as a whole, its largest operating group, its largest operating division, or other operating divisions.

responsibility for both product and workplace safety. In addition, OSHA is *the* premier law in workplace-safety matters; all manufacturers are subject to OSHA workplace standards in one way or another.

In some instances, a safety unit's involvement with *work* safety issues is so extensive that its organizational positioning is dictated by OSHA-related reporting requirements. In one metals company, for example, the *product* safety group is reportedly "overshadowed" by the metal producer's *work* safety group—with occupational-safety issues being of paramount concern. The two-person product-safety unit is appended to the much larger occupational-safety unit.

The Environmental Protection Act is another statute to which product-safety administrators must frequently pay close attention. When products can have an environmental impact, this will usually require the attention of a company's product-safety executives. The Environmental Protection Agency may act to disapprove the use of a particular ingredient or device because of its alleged deleterious impact on the environment (as it has, for example, in regulating the use of mercury pesticides in water-based paints, fluorocarbon propellants for aerosols, noisy lawn mowers, etc.), or a class of product, such as asbestos or some other carcinogen, may be directly affected by EPA regulation.

Other product safety statutes, cited by manufacturers, include the Consumer Products Safety Act; the Food, Drug and Cosmetic Act; and the Hazardous Substances Act. The Consumer Products Safety Act, perhaps because of its omnibus nature, ranks high among the laws of concern to safety professionals. Even among manufacturers whose products are marketed solely to industrial users, a quarter describe themselves as affected by the Consumer Products Safety Act. As noted earlier, many of these companies do produce components or materials that are, in turn, used by makers of consumer products and the manufacturers are thus subject, in an indirect fashion, to the provisions of the CPSA.

In several instances, enactment of the Consumer Products Safety Act not only affected the organization of companies' safety efforts, but was, in fact, *responsible* for initiating it. Until the passage of CPSA, several of the firms surveyed had no product-safety functions whatever—either formal or informal. Then, confronted with the reporting requirements of the Act (particularly Section 15-B), and the legal need to develop product-safety standards, companies were motivated to appoint safety specialists.

One Company's Product-Safety Programs—International Telephone and Telegraph Corporation

International Telephone & Telegraph, one of the largest multinational corporations, has nearly 375,000 employees located in 70 countries around the world. During the past decade, ITT management has moved to standardize the way the company's various divisions and subsidiaries handle issues such as consumer affairs and product safety.

Like nearly every other manufacturer, various units of ITT have, from time to time, become involved in product-safety incidents which have proved costly to both the company and its customers. It was important, ITT management believed, to acquaint divisional and subsidiary management with the fact that liability insurance was not a satisfactory hedge against losses resulting from product-safety incidents.

A company executive pointed out that any firm's operating units can be lulled into a sense of complacency, believing that their liability insurance will reimburse them for financial losses resulting from product-safety problems. But insurance carriers principally service claims, and a firm eventually has to pay back these costs, on an experience basis. The executive went on to say product recalls are not covered by insurance at all. In reality, the cost of recall comes directly and immediately out of these companies' pockets.

The present price for product-safety mistakes, plus the potential for even greater penalties in the future, led ITT's management to organize a company-wide product-safety management system. During early 1973, it was decided to create a corporate-level consumer affairs function. This function was made a part of the corporate quality department (see Exhibit 20) and was where product-safety responsibilities were first vested.

The consumer-affairs function was given the responsibility for developing guidelines for product-safety management and promoting product- safety improvement programs—also, for coordinating actions in hazardous product situations and product recall campaigns.

One of the first tasks of the consumer-affairs unit was to provide a definitive policy on product safety. A policy entitled "Safety of ITT Products" (Exhibit 16) was approved by management and distributed to the heads of all ITT units. Then, a corporate-level Product Safety Council, composed of representatives of quality, legal, technical, marketing, manufacturing, insurance, medical, safety and fire prevention, and other appropriate product line managers and staff members, was established.

Operating Unit Involvement

The head of each operating unit was asked by management to appoint a member of his immediate staff to serve as a product-safety coordinator. They were also instructed to establish a product-safety review board with representatives from the unit's engineering, manufacturing, quality, legal, and marketing functions. The primary purpose of the review boards was to keep a close eye on the product-safety situation in that particular unit.

Provisions of the ITT company policy on product safety state, "If an unreasonably hazardous product situation exists, or *is suspected* [emphasis added] the general manager or managing director (of the unit) will immediately notify the legal representative on the unit's product-safety review board in a legal confidential form requesting legal advice. The legal representative will immediately advise the director—consumer and environmental affairs of ITT—on the facts and legal questions and at the same time the product-safety coordinator will take any

emergency steps necessary to minimize the risk of injury to any user."

The ITT policy also requires that each unit's product-safety review board prepare a Product Safety Compliance Manual for its products, and that it conduct a yearly product-safety system audit.

In the course of implementing this policy, the director of consumer and enviornmental affairs, sent a memorandum to all units (Exhibit 17) asking them to conform to the new policy statement and to provide the corporate office of consumer affairs with the names of their product-safety coordinators. This memo was accompanied by pertinent product-safety guidelines and an invitation for the unit to be represented at a product-safety seminar to be held in convenient locations throughout the United States and Europe.

Within a relatively short period of time, most of the ITT units had complied with the latter request. Typically, each unit had set up a four- or five-member review board, comprised of general management, legal, manufacturing, technical and quality executives.

The next stage in the corporate-wide safety program was to design a product-safety audit. Exhibits 18 and 19 illustrate some of the questions contained in a 34-page audit developed for operating unit use.

These safety audits were reviewed by the units' legal counsels. In some instances, the units may have had too sketchy a grasp of their product-safety responsibilities—particularly with regard to the safety laws and regulations that applied to the unit and its products. In other instances, however, the audits showed that the divisions' executives were acutely aware of their safety responsibilities and already had an embryonic product-safety program underway.

In addition to the safety audit, the units regularly conduct risk analyses of their products to make certain these products are reasonably safe (for their intended use and foreseeable misuse and abuse). The methods used include devices such as Fault Tree Analysis and Profile Analysis, techniques found useful because they provide a means for quantifying safety as a product parameter.

Positioning the Product-Safety Function

Like the consumer affairs function, the corporate level product-safety function at ITT reports to the vice president of corporate quality—a position directly responsible to the office of the chief executive (see Exhibit 28).

The logic for this arrangement is stated as:

"1. It provides product safety with a direct channel to quality assurance for problem analysis and corrective action.

"2. The quality department has a long history of close and effective collaboration with technical, manufacturing, and legal staffs of the company.

"3. It also provides product safety with a direct line to the office of the chief executive, thus assuring its independence."

The corporate Product Safety Council, as well as the individual product safety-coordinators in each operating unit, report on a dotted-line basis to the product safety director in the corporate quality assurance department.

The corporate product-safety function is intended to act primarily as a monitoring and coordinating one. Since the department is relatively small, the bulk of the firm's product-safety effort must necessarily originate in and be conducted by division- or unit-level executives.

Product-Safety Improvement Programs

As part of the overall plan to decentralize the product-safety responsibilities, ITT management instructed each unit to develop, as soon as possible, a "product-safety improvement program." The goal of such programs was to identify the sources of product-safety problems and develop policies and techniques to surmount such problems. Typically, the program focused on factors such as product design, testing, processing, material substitutions, quality-assurance standards, and so forth. But it also looked at procedural factors, such as quality-assurance controls, cost reduction compromises, and the adequacy of use instructions and labelling.

ITT safety executives, viewing product-safety difficulties encountered at other firms, decided that one of the most common causes of product claims is a product's physical features—particularly those that may produce difficulties resulting from compromising good, substantial functional design for more attractive visual appeals. Physical features, such as sculptured corners, edges, and obstructions based on visual considerations alone, present unnecessary hazards to the consumer. While the aesthetic quality of some of these designs cannot be denied, ITT safety specialists point out that companies must exercise discipline in safety judgment to eliminate such exposures.

In addition, ITT safety executives recognize that many firms' products are designed "from the outside in"—a situation that can result in inadequate construction when coupled with inadequate design testing which fails to duplicate "real life" product usage. When such an approach is followed, product-liability risks are likely to be multiplied several times over. As an example, an appliance might be tested using a lower cost housing material. The testing likely would be conducted in an air-conditioned laboratory. Later, when appliances using this housing are subjected to tropical temperature and use conditions, the housing might distort and shrink, exposing live electrical components. In such an instance, an extensive product replacement program would have to be initiated.

A company safety executive recalls that in one firm an operating unit's purchasing agent obtained a large number of power cords, for a floor polishing machine, at bargain prices, and then had these cords substituted without the benefit of a complete engineering evaluation. Only after an accident was it discovered that the color coding on the bargain power cords was reversed—greatly increasing the chances of an accident.

There is an awareness that there are continuing temptations for raw material or component substitutions, in order to lower production costs. Thus, ITT safety executives must continually scrutinize such practices. They recognize that some substitutions might be made without fully considering what impact these changes may have on a product's safety characteristics. At ITT, product-safety evaluation (as part of the required formal product qualification and requalification procedure in each unit) is said to have reduced the possibilities for such ill-considered substitutions.

In addition, management is kept fully informed about the status of a unit's product-safety program in a special section of the unit's quality status report as prepared on a monthly basis in accordance with a corporate-wide standard practice.

A Matter of Planning

Given the scale of its operations, and the diversity of products manufactured, ITT management knows that during any single year the company may have to recall some of its products because of safety considerations. This reality has prompted the company to require, as part of its safety organizational program, standby recall programs in each unit.

As a company spokesperson points out, products might be recalled for any number of reasons other than strict safety considerations, e.g., failure to meet advertised performance standards, evidence of incorrect or inadequate labelling, and so forth. The company's divisions, however, are expected to treat all recalls seriously because product recalls, overall, have been found to have a significantly higher impact on corporate profits than even product-liability lawsuits. This is because, in addition to the immediate direct costs of repair, reimbursement and replacement, must be added the intangible costs of inconvenience and damage to product integrity and customer loyalty (not to mention the ultimate costs of restrictive legislation or regulations that might be prompted by recall incidents).

Effective product recall planning requires that operating units prepare specific standby action plans. This program involves the listing of recall criteria and the development of a liaison function with the corporate staff, particularly in ·the case of national or international recall campaigns.

An ITT executive explains that the emphasis is on advance planning: "We know that no matter how quality conscious our people may be, product safety situations will arise. Advance planning can do a great deal to mitigate or reduce the impact of such situations on both customers and the company."

A Quality Cost System

In order to measure the contribution of its product-safety effort, ITT has, for more than a decade, emphasized what is referred to internally as a *quality cost system*. This system requires the comptroller in each operating unit to be able to "pinpoint" the cost of quality. This assessment includes such things as the amount and cost of scrap and rework done at a particular plant; the cost of products returned because of faulty design or construction; the cost of product-liability claims and settlements; the cost of product recalls; the cost of field modifications made, and so forth.

According to an ITT spokesman, once such costs are identified and measured, the management of an operating unit can see for itself the cost of nonconformance. Then, management is much more inclined to take necessary remedial action. The assumption is that the total cost of quality in a manufacturing operation should run between four and six percent of the unit's total sales dollars. But the true cost of quality—the cost of not maintaining safe products—might run in some companies as high as 15 or 20 percent of total sales (or more). ITT management estimates that its quality cost system has saved the company as much as $50 million during one recent year and, in aggregate, well over $500 million during the past decade.

Local Responsibility

Throughout the firm's safety programs, attention has been given to providing each operating unit with the responsibility as well as the tools for managing its own product-safety effort. But at the same time, each unit is kept well aware that the corporate Product Safety Council will be overseeing the implementation of the unit's product-safety program, recall campaigns, and so forth.

"Product safety," a company safety executive explains, "is another product responsibility that requires planned management actions. If we do the job right, and implement product safety programs that are effective, the added costs will be negligible compared to the completely unpredictable costs associated with product liability suits and recalls. All the tools are available; all it takes is management commitment."

Exhibit 15: Appointment of Product-Safety Coordinator—International Telephone and Telegraph Corporation

Ernest W. Karlin
Director
Consumer and Environmental Affairs

International Telephone and
Telegraph Corporation

World Headquarters

320 Park Avenue
New York N.Y. 10022
Telephone (212) 752-6000

Subject: a) Appointment of a Product Safety Coordinator
             b) Quality College Seminar – Product Safety & Liability
                Prevention

Reference: ITT Policy QU 14.0 – "Safety of ITT Products"

Dear

We appreciate your cooperation in appointing
Product Safety Coordinator for your Unit.

The referenced policy on product safety requires that some specific
actions be taken in each ITT Unit. Two of the most important are:

1. Implementation of a product safety improvement program, and

2. Establishing the mechanism for dealing with substantially
   hazardous problems that might arise.

To provide your Product Safety Coordinator with the "know-how"
and reference material needed to carry out this policy we have been conducting
a series of orientation seminars.

The first one in Europe took place June 30/July 1 in Brussels. The
only other one presently planned in your geographic area will be in
on November   (program enclosed). I strongly urge you to send your
Product Safety Coordinator to this seminar.

Please complete and return the enclosed reservation questionnaire
by October 25 so that we will have sufficient lead time for necessary
arrangements.

Thank you for your consideration.

Sincerely,

Ernest W. Karlin

Enc.

ITT POLICY GUIDE	SUBJECT	**POLICY**	NUMBER QU 14.0
		SAFETY OF ITT PRODUCTS	EFFECTIVE
			CANCELS
AFFECTS ITT SYSTEM	SIGNATURE *Philip B Crosby* VICE PRESIDENT & DIRECTOR-QUALITY-ITT		DATED
			PAGE 1 OF 2

INTENT

It is the intent of this Policy to assure that the products of ITT System units are safe and in compliance with all applicable laws, regulations and standards established for the protection of users of such products.

SCOPE

This Policy applies to all ITT System units who manufacture, import, export, sell or distribute products.

DEFINITION OF TERMS

- Hazard

  Source of risk, which is inherently capable of inflicting harm or creating a loss.

- Risk

  The foreseeable or predictable amount of harm likely to result from the hazard.

- Risk of Injury

  A risk of personal injury, severe or frequent illness, or death.

- Unreasonably Hazardous

  An unreasonably hazardous product is a product which contains one or more characteristics of design, manufacture, application, labelling, etc., which raises a risk to the user he could not know or foresee, and which involves possible personal injury, severe or frequent illness, or death.

Exhibit 17: Announcement of Product-Safety Program—International Telephone and Telegraph Corporation

RESPONSIBILITY

The General Manager or Managing Director of each ITT System unit is responsible for the implementation of a product safety and liability prevention program responsive to applicable laws, regulations and standards. An ITT system unit shall not manufacture, import, export, sell or distribute any product which is deemed unreasonably hazardous.

The Director-Consumer and Environmental Affairs-ITT is responsible for the coordination of corporate efforts directed in accordance with the intent and requirements of this Policy, and will act as Chairman of the Corporate Product Safety Council composed of senior members of Quality, Legal, Technical, Marketing, Manufacturing, Insurance, Medical, Safety and Fire Prevention, appropriate Product Line Managers and other staffs.

APPLICATION

- The effective application of this Policy requires that the unit General Manager or Managing Director appoint a member of his staff to act as the Product Safety Coordinator and a Product Safety Review Board composed of senior representatives from Engineering, Manufacturing, Quality, Legal, Marketing, and other applicable functions to develop, implement and oversee a product safety improvement program. The Product Safety Coordinator is the contact between the unit and the Corporate Product Safety Council.

- If an "unreasonably hazardous product" situation exists or is suspected, the General Manager or Managing Director will immediately notify the Legal representative on the unit Product Safety Review Board in legal confidential form requesting legal advice. The Legal representative will immediately advise the Director-Consumer and Environmental Affairs-ITT on the facts and legal questions. At the same time, the Product Safety Coordinator will take any emergency steps necessary to minimize risk of injury to any user.

  The unit Product Safety Review Board will expeditiously develop a corrective action plan and after approval by the Corporate Product Safety Council will oversee its implementation.

- Each unit will prepare a Product Safety Compliance Manual responsive to applicable laws, regulations and standards and assure that a comprehensive product safety audit is conducted at least once a year.

- Should a General Manager or Managing Director deem this Policy to be not applicable to his operation, he may apply (through appropriate Group Headquarters) to the Director-Consumer and Environmental Affairs-ITT for exemption.

Exhibit 18: Product-Safety Audit Sheet—International Telephone and Telegraph Corporation

ITT PRODUCT SAFETY SYSTEM AUDIT

UNIT ______ AUDITOR ______

LOCATION ______ DATE ______ P ___ OF ___

ITEM	EXPLANATORY NOTES	RATING 1	RATING 2	RATING 3	RATING 4	RATING 5	Function Responsible: CONS. AFFAIRS	Function Responsible: QUALITY	Function Responsible: ADMIN.			COMMENTS
1.0 MANAGEMENT CONSIDERATIONS 1.1 Is the Unit familiar with ITT Policy QU 14.0, "Safety of ITT Products" - and its requirements? Yes___ No___												
1.2 Has the unit appointed a Product Safety Coordinator and a Product Safety Review Board? Yes___ No___ ______ ______ Name - Product Safety Coord. Title												
1.3 Has the unit prepared a list of major products and the applicable regulations and standards? Yes___ No___												
1.4 Has the unit prepared a Product Safety Compliance Manual responsive to applicable laws, regulations and standards? Yes___ No___												
1.5 Does the unit have written standards, procedures and specifications addressed to safety aspects of new product design? Yes___ No___ If yes, list the source of these documents (i.e., Federal Industry, Trade Association, UL, ITT, etc.) ______ ______ ______												

Exhibit 19: Product-Safety Audit Sheet—International Telephone and Telegraph Corporation

ITT PRODUCT SAFETY SYSTEM AUDIT

UNIT _____ AUDITOR _____

LOCATION _____ DATE _____ P ___ OF ___

ITEM	EXPLANATORY NOTES	RATING					Function Responsible			COMMENTS
		1	2	3	4	5	CONS. AFFAIRS	QUALITY	ADMIN.	
1.6 Does the unit include USER safety considerations in the design of its products and services. If yes, by what mechanisms. _____										
1.7 Does the unit maintain records of personal injury or property damage related to its products and services? Yes___ No___										
1.8 Does the unit include Product Safety proof-testing as part of its New Product Qualification Test/Product Release procedures? Yes___ No___										
1.9 Does the unit have the laboratory and personnel capability to perform all necessary Product Safety proof tests? Yes___ No___ If no, describe how and where these tests are performed. _____										
1.10 If the unit had to recall a portion of some product, could that portion be traced and found without recalling all of the product? Yes___ No___										

Exhibit 20: Product-Safety Organizational Chart—International Telephone and Telegraph Corporation

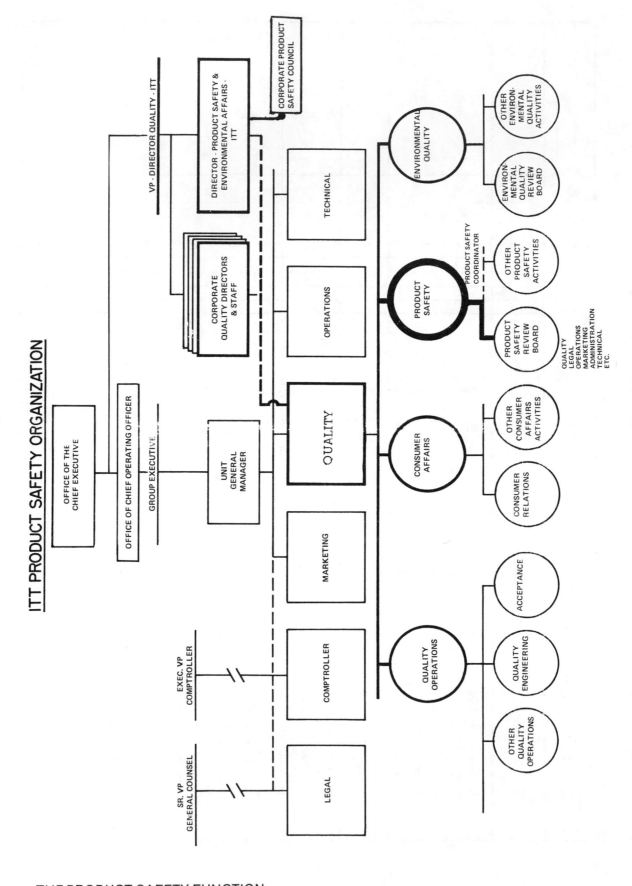

ITT PRODUCT SAFETY ORGANIZATION

Chapter 3

Intradepartmental Organizational Variations

IN RELATIVELY FEW of the firms studied is there a "full-fledged" product-safety department—that is, a unit with several different persons, subunits, and so forth. But in a few firms there are sufficiently large staffs and subdivisions so as to provide an opportunity to examine the intradepartmental organizational variations that exist in product-safety units.

The most common ways of establishing staff assignments, and dividing the work load in full-time product-safety units, are:

(1) Primarily on the basis of professional specialization;

(2) Primarily on the basis of the functional elements of the product-safety job; and

(3) Primarily on the basis of product and user categories.

Division by Professional Specialists

The work loads of the product-safety unit can be organized around the separate professional specialties required by the unit, with staff specialists given responsibilities for all matters involving their particular specialties. This division of responsibility is most often found at the corporate level in multidivision manufacturing companies.

In the hypothetical example shown in Exhibit 21, the product-safety organization might require the services of a toxicologist, a human factors engineer, an ecologist, and an analytical chemist. When product-safety issues arise in such a company's divisions, the product-safety director could call on each of the professionals on the staff to analyze and report on the issue from his or her professional viewpoint. The safety executive would then coordinate the input received from these professional investigations.

For example, suppose a customer using agricultural spray equipment made by one of the company's divisions, and a dangerous insecticide made by another, were accidentally to cause the insecticide to be dumped into a freshwater stream. The product-safety director could mobilize the four relevant staff specialists and develop solutions to the dilemma.

The toxicologist, for example, could focus on the impact the insecticide might have on humans drinking the water or eating fish contaminated by the insecticide. The ecologist could examine the deleterious impact the concentration of insecticide might have on marine life in the stream, aquatic vegetation, and so on. The human factors engineer could examine the accident itself, focusing on how and why the customer came to misuse the firm's equipment,

Exhibit 21: Intradepartmental Organization by Professional Specialization

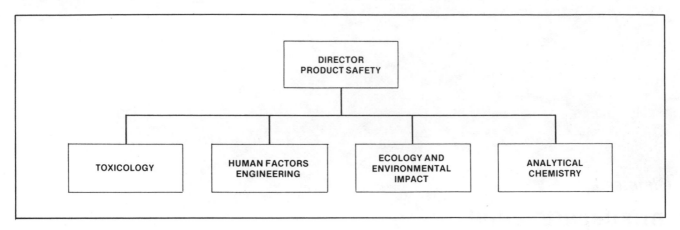

failed to follow product use instructions on the insecticide, and so forth. The analytical chemist could provide support by helping to identify the concentration of insecticide at the point where the accident occurred, as well as other points downstream.

In the example cited above, the product-safety director functions as a coordinator for the various professional specialists in the safety unit. The executive defines the problem in broad terms, correlates the group's research findings, and distills the recommendations of the safety professionals in a report to management.

Of course, it is not necessary for such product-safety specialists to be full-time staff members of a safety unit. In some firms, essentially the same result is obtained by drawing upon the part-time services of specialists assigned regularly to other departments.

Variation by Functional Elements of the Product-Safety Responsibility

In some firms, the product-safety unit primarily audits the safety characteristics of products at various manufacturing stages, ranging from raw materials to finished goods. And the division of work in such units may reflect these functional variations. This variety

Exhibit 22: Intradepartmental Organization by Functional Elements of Safety Task

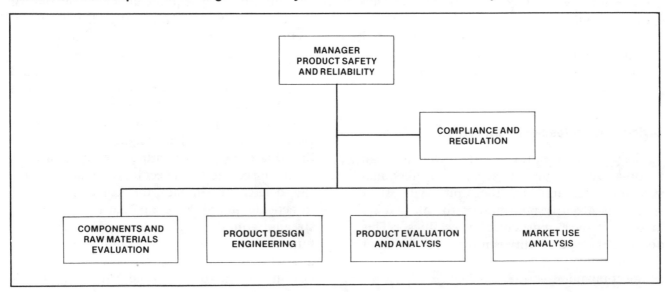

of organizational structure is most often found at the division level, or among nondivisionalized firms.

Again, in a hypothetical example, a safety unit's tasks might begin with the evaluation of raw materials and components that make up a product—not simply from a quality assurance standpoint, but as a matter of measuring product reliability, conformance with applicable state or federal specifications, avoidance of component or materials substitution, and so forth.

But there may also be individuals within this same product-safety unit who focus on who the product is designed, with the goal of eliminating or modifying those product characteristics which are now, or could in the future, be sources of injuries. Such specialists would examine the stress resistance of a product, from a design standpoint, its reliability or useful life characteristics, and so on, and make these findings available to management and to other staff members of the safety unit concerned with product evaluation and analysis.

The latter staffers—those concerned with product evaluation and analysis—might be given the task of examining existing products which have been the target of safety complaints and evaluating how these products perform under various customer use conditions. In this hypothetical example, these members of the unit's safety staff could try to forecast where failures might occur and their efforts could be buttressed by market use specialists who could examine how various products are used in the field and the risks associated with different uses and misuses.

In this variety of workload division, the product-safety staff is segregated according to fairly well-defined functional responsibilities. It might happen that these responsibilities are coincident with various stages of a product's development and marketing. But it is also likely that the division of labor would take into account different kinds of analysis and investigation which may, or may not, be coincident with a product's maturation from prototype to commercial reality.

Variance by Product User Categories

It is also possible to divide product-safety responsibilities according to the type of customer or market. In the theoretical example shown in Exhibit 23, a product-safety specialist is assigned to each of four different classes of customers. Such an assignment could reflect the nature of the product, as well as the customer. For example, a "professional products" specialist might be assigned the task of handling safety issues for that unit of the company manufacturing and marketing a medical device or medical instruments. This specialist would have an entirely different set of professional qualifications from those of the staff member in charge of dealing with safety issues for hardware products and handtools. By the same token, the staff member assigned to an industrial products group could be expected to have a greater knowledge of occupational safety characteristics and how the firm's products might be affected by such considerations.

The organizational arrangement shown in Exhibit 23 could exist in a nondivisionalized company, or perhaps at the corporate level of a multidivisional firm in which safety responsibilities are highly centralized. In the latter case, each of the specialists or groups in the unit would be assigned to the appropriate divisions and their salaries and expenses charged back to these divisions.

Organizational Realities

In a majority of cases where there is a product-safety unit large enough to warrant study of its intradepartmental organization, it will be found that the unit's tasks are most likely to be divided by professional specialization. However, relatively few of the units examined are "pure" in that they conform exactly to one of the three previously described organizational arrangements. More often, there is a preponderance of one type of arrangement or another, but with one or two "deviations" from the models described.

For example, one firm has a corporate-level

Exhibit 23: Intradepartmental Organization by Product User Categories

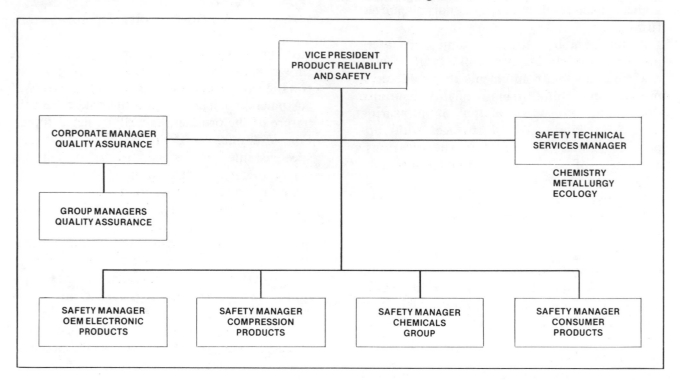

product-safety unit that is primarily organized on a professional specialization basis. But it also includes one staff member who is a "regulatory specialist"—an engineer-attorney who spends all of his efforts examining the nature and impact of various state and federal safety regulations. This staff member acts as an internal consultant to other professionals of the safety unit, providing advice and data on specific safety statutes. And in another company, as also illustrated in Exhibit 23, the safety unit can be primarily organized by product and customer categories, but the executive heading this unit is assisted by a staff specialist who provides engineering and analytical services of value to both the executive and to the safety managers for the various products and customer-use categories.

Deciding on the Degree of Product Safety

Underlying many of the considerations that managements must weigh, in deciding how to structure their companies' safety activities, is the question: How safe must our product be? And the corollary is: How can we measure the degree of safety?

None of the safety executives surveyed had a wholly satisfactory answer to either of these questions. A number of them expressed their belief that their firms must concentrate on measuring *risk* rather than safety. But this creates further semantic difficulties because risk to the individual user of the product is not always coincident with risk to the company. For example, there may be little physical risk to some consumers, as a result of a certain safety miscue, but the adverse publicity, impact of regulatory agency investigations, and so on, may pose substantial economic risks to the firm. Conversely, the risk to the user may be of serious (physical) proportions, whereas the company, because of its size or insurance protection, would experience relatively modest (financial) risk from a safety-defective product.

One safety researcher, preparing a study for a Committee on Science and Public Policy of the National Academy of Sciences on the scientific basis—and limitations—of the determination of safety, has stated:

"We [the research team] deliberately avoided the word "safety" altogether [in drafting the report], because of its vagueness and long history of misuse. Safety is not measured. *Risks* are measured. Only when those risks are weighed on the balance of social values, can safety be judged: *A thing is safe if attendant risks are judged to be acceptable.*"[1]

Increasingly, companies are finding ways to measure some dimensions of the risks they—and users of their products—face. By analyzing customer complaints, by assiduous product testing, and so forth, they can at least estimate the empirical probability that a product will cause harm—and they can perhaps even gauge the severity of injury that might result. Obviously, very few—if any—products are risk-free: And even knowing the statistical incidence of accidents involving the product does not solve the problem. The more difficult task is that of judging whether or not the determined level of risk to the company, without further corrective action, is acceptable on legal, political, moral and economic grounds. Further, what may have been "acceptable" in the recent past—in terms of potential risk and injury—may no longer be acceptable. According to an observer in one safety-regulatory agency: "Companies' myopic endorsement of what were previously acceptable levels of risk must certainly be regarded as one of the primary factors behind the safety difficulties in which many firms now find themselves embroiled."

A concern of a number of corporate safety officials surveyed is that both the benefits and safety risks associated with product design, composition of products, or methods of use be well discussed, in advance, inside the company. That is one reason given for the formation of some companies' product safety committees (see page 84). It has also been an important consideration, several executives state, in their managements' designation of a single individual or department to deal with product-safety matters.

"Product safety professionals tend to be more conservative and less willing to accept product risks than their executive counterparts in marketing, research and development, and so on," one metals company executive claims. "They know we can't make our products absolutely safe, but they seem to be much less willing to expand the risk ratio than are other executives whose departmental or divisional interests may be involved in a risk decision...and we see this reluctance as a desirable trait."

On the other hand, it has sometimes been charged that governmental safety regulators are too often unresponsive to the economic and practical limits of safety. An executive of the Council on Wage and Price Stability, for example, has made this observation in criticizing the Consumer Products Safety Commission: "We are aware of the difficulties involved in the application of cost-benefit analysis, especially in matters relating to injury and loss of life. These difficulties are especially apparent in attempting to measure benefits when these benefits are in the form of decreased risk of injury or loss of life, and we make no attempt to gloss over the very real problems involved. Nevertheless, we need to know what we are getting when we invest in increased safety, either by placing reasonable values on these intangible benefits, or, if that is not feasible, simply by estimating the number of different types of injuries that would be prevented. Even given such limitations, we believe that a cost-benefit framework can be helpful in deciding whether, in fact, society would be better off by the adoption of a given proposal. In our opinion, the Consumer Products Safety Commission has not, in the past, been sufficiently sensitive to the usefulness of the cost-benefit framework."[2]

[1]William W. Lowrance, *Of Acceptable Risk: Science and the Determination of Safety.* Los Altos, California; William Kaufman, Inc., 1976, p. 75.

[2]Statement on behalf of The Council on Wage and Price Stability, by Thomas M. Leonard, economist, before the Consumer Products Safety Advisory Council, August 17, 1976.

Chapter 4

Reporting Relationships and Job Titles of Product-Safety Executives

KNOWING to whom a functional executive reports, and where a particular department is positioned in the organizational matrix, often provides clues to the significance that companies accord that function. But this is not a handy barometer with which to gauge the importance that companies accord product-safety responsibilities.

As already noted, a majority of all product-safety activities are conducted on a part-time basis. And most of these part-time arrangements are found at the operating level. Perhaps the most significance variation in reporting relationships is observable between those companies that have full-time product-safety functions and those that fulfill these responsibilities on a part-time basis.

About two-thirds *full-time* product-safety functions report to a "functional" executive, usually the manager of the company's research and development, engineering or quality-assurance departments (see Table 6). The remaining third report either directly to the president or to the executive vice president. But, as shown in Table 7, part-time product-safety executives, in nondivisionalized firms, are more likely to report to a general executive, usually the vice president or general manager of their operating unit. This is less so for divisionalized companies, but as an observer proceeds downward through the organizational pyramid—from corporate to division-level responsibilities—it is much more likely that the product-safety function, on either a full or part-time basis, will also be reporting to a general management executive. Usually, this executive is in charge of the group or division. In those instances in which the product-safety specialist reports to other than such an executive, it is most likely that he will be responsible to a quality assurance, research and development, or engineering executive.

As noted earlier, the vast majority of those companies surveyed have product-safety functions (either on a full- or part-time basis) present at both a corporate and operating unit level—that is, they are neither fully centralized nor decentralized as far as product-safety arrangements are concerned. In these firms, it is often difficult to generalize about the reporting relationships of the safety executives. Factors such as the size of the organization, the existence—or lack of—specialized functions such as quality assurance, engineering, and so on, can determine to whom the safety-executive reports. In nondivisionalized firms, which are usually smaller in size than their divisionalized counterparts, about a third of the full-time executives, and a majority of the part-time executives, will report to either the company president or executive vice president.

In those instances in which the full-time

Table 6: Reporting Relationships for Full-Time Product-Safety Functions

Executive to Whom Full-Time Product-Safety Function Reports	In Nondivisionalized Companies	In Divisionalized Companies		
		At Corporate Level	At Group Level	At Major Division Level
General Executive	33%	23%	59%	53%
President	20	23	—	—
Executive Vice President	13	—	—	—
Divisional or Group Vice President	—	—	59	53
Functional Executive	67	77	41	47
Research and development	13	23	3	3
Engineering	13	—	7	16
Quality assurance	—	8	—	8
Administration	7	7	—	—
Production	—	—	—	13
Other functional executive[1]	34	40	31	8
Total	100%	100%	100%	100%

[1]Includes executives in sales, finance, personnel or insurance functions.
Note: Details do not necessarily add to totals because of rounding.

Table 7: Reporting Relationships for Persons with Part-Time Product-Safety Responsibilities

Executive to Whom Person with Part-Time Product-Safety Responsibility Reports	In Nondivisionalized Companies	In Divisionalized Companies		
		At Corporate Level	At Group Level	At Major Division Level
General Executive	71%	48%	74%	69%
President	54	31	—	—
Executive Vice President	17	17	—	—
Divisional or Group Vice President	—	—	74	69
Functional Executive	29	52	26	31
Research and development	—	—	—	—
Engineering	21	—	5	4
Quality assurance	—	8	2	3
Administration	4	—	2	4
Production	—	—	—	—
Other functional executive[1]	4	43	17	16
Total	100%	100%	100%	100%

[1]Includes executives in sales, finance, personnel or insurance functions.
Note: Details do not necessarily add to totals because of rounding.

safety executive does not report to the company president, it is likely that the function is filled by staff specialists in either the engineering or quality assurance departments of the company and reports through the executives of those departments. If the function is performed on part-time basis, it could similarly report through such a unit, but might also be handled as one of the responsibilities of a staff executive such as the director of quality assurance.

The Effect of Occupational Safety Considerations

One other factor of note, as far as product-safety reporting relationships are concerned, involves the matter of occupational safety. As will be shown later, it is not unusual for product safety and occupational safety to be combined. Such a configuration can affect the reporting relationship of the product-safety specialist, particularly since occupational health and safety functions may—most particularly at a corporate level—report through a personnel or employee relations department.

At the operating unit level, however, the safety function, regardless of whether it is combined with occupational health and safety, most likely reports to the general manager of the operating unit—and thus is little different from those functions that are not combined with occupational health and safety.

Other Reporting Relationships

There is no shortage whatever of places to which the product-safety function can report. Among the companies studied, safety executives are found reporting to such disparate offices as the vice president of administration, vice president of customer relations, and so forth. In only a few instances, however, do safety executives report to marketing or sales departments. When such an arrangement does exist, it is most likely found at the group level of the organizational pyramid.

Job Titles of Product-Safety Executives

In relatively few of the firms studied is there an executive whose job title includes the words "product-safety." Naturally, those many individuals who perform product-safety functions on a part-time basis do not have a job title with the term product safety in it. But even among those firms where there is an executive performing product-safety functions on a full-time basis, it is not certain that the job title will reflect these responsibilities. Companies may, for example, choose to describe the function as one of product reliability, quality assurance, and so forth.

Companies may well regard themselves as having a "full-time product-safety executive"—whether or not any individual bears such a job title. This creates the somewhat confusing situation in which firms first report that they have a "full-time safety executive" and then describe a job title which does not clearly reflect such a responsibility.

Complicating the situation further is the fact that product-safety responsibilities in other companies are regarded as the part-time duties of the director of quality assurance, research and development, or engineering. But the executives heading these functions, in fulfilling product-safety responsibilities on a "part-time" basis, may, in fact, have one or more members of their staff working on safety issues on a full-time basis. Again, however, these staff members' job titles may not necessarily reflect safety responsibilities. More likely, they will reflect the professional specialization of the individuals—engineering, chemistry or whatever. This type of situation also develops among those companies having occupational health and safety units which have, among their staffs, specialists concerned with *product* safety.

Identifying the Product-Safety Executive

At one stage in the Board's survey, the names of product-safety executives in selected companies were sought for possible interview. To obtain these names, telephone calls were made to 127 large companies (all members of the *Fortune 500* list) with corporate headquarters located in the corridor between Boston and Washington.

The telephone interviewer, a Cornell University intern working under Conference Board supervision, first asked the switchboard operator in each case for "the name of the individual in charge of product safety," and then asked to be connected to that person. If the operator was unable to identify anyone at any level in the company having responsibility for product-safety matters, the interviewer then asked to be transferred to the firm's personnel or public relations department to pursue the search further.

The probe suggests that an outsider who tried to reach a manufacturer by telephone, with a question or complaint regarding product safety, might have substantial trouble getting through to the right party. The results of these telephone contacts are summarized below.

•Telephone operators in most of the companies had no idea who in the firm is in charge of product safety.

•Usually, it was necessary to talk with at least three persons in a company before the individual in charge of product safety could be identified. In some cases, ten different individuals were approached before it could be established who in the firm might have product-safety responsibilities.

•Even in some organizations known to have active, full-time product-safety units, the personnel and public relations departments in these companies were not strongly aware of their existence.

Chapter 5

Organizational Relationship Between Work and Product Safety

IT IS common practice, for the same company unit to oversee both work safety and product safety. But among the executives questioned—including those whose own companies combine the functions—there is widespread preference for separating them. Nevertheless, there is also a widespread belief that decisions on combining or separating product safety and work safety are appropriately dependent on individual company circumstances.

The Case for Separation

Several reasons are offered for possible separation of work-safety and product-safety assignments. Typically, executives see work safety and product safety as having "relatively little in common," and requiring different kinds of background, training, skills and expertise. Some judge each of the two areas as being so broad and specialized as to make their combination a needless union between two disparate tasks and responsibilities. The enactment of the Occupational Safety and Health Act of 1970 (OSHA) is said to have exacerbated the differences. The recordkeeping, reporting and inspection requirements of OSHA have created safety specialists oriented almost wholly to workplace—not marketplace—concerns.

Further, the executives state, work safety is necessarily the concern of internally-oriented functions, such as the personnel department, plant engineering, or production. By contrast, they point out, product safety is, to a large extent, more logically oriented to forces and factors outside the company. It necessitates, for example, a concern for the customers' situations, and the reactions of designers, marketers and quality assurance specialists to safety issues.

What is possible, or even appropriate from an organizational standpoint, depends, of course, on the kinds of products whose safety is at issue, as well as the company level at which safety responsibilities must be met. The spokesman for a metals company, in which each division possesses substantial operating autonomy, says that it might be possible to combine each division's work and product-safety responsibilities. On the other hand, the executive is concerned that it would be difficult to create such a mixed function at a corporate level. He notes, too, that while some of the firm's divisions have no serious product-safety worries, all are concerned with work-safety matters.

In other instances, differences in safety regulations for products and workers sometimes have a pivotal impact on decisions as to whether or not work-safety and product-safety tasks should be joined. Some safety executives note that the federal OSHA requirements, as well as numerous work-safety strictures established by states, require the kind of routine reporting and liaison activities that can often be managed without difficulty by company units such as personnel, insurance and the like.

By contrast, they point out that many of the statutes dealing with product safety (excepting principally the Food, Drug and Cosmetic Act) tend to require "exception" actions. Provisions of the Consumer Product Safety Act and the Hazardous Substances Act, for example, may require reporting or affirmative activity only when an unsafe product possibility is discovered.

It is suggested, as well, that potential hazards involving work safety are generally more readily recognized—by management and other employees—and often can be planned for and dealt with in a more direct manner than can product-safety hazards. The latter may arise not from anything so apparent as a defect in product design, but from unanticipated misuse, or a misunderstanding of the product's capabilities or characteristics by the company's customers. It is far more difficult, safety specialists say, to anticipate and forestall such contingencies.

In essence, the different approaches required, and possibly the different kinds of personnel needed to accomplish these tasks, are seen as being so different as to substantiate the need, in these executives' views, for separate organizational arrangements.

The Case for Combination

By contrast, a number of executives consider work-safety and product-safety tasks to be mutually reinforcing. In their experience, bringing these functions together facilitates the necessary coordination between safety activities in the company, while avoiding costly overlapping and duplication of safety-related functions. A single safety unit, as they see it, better provides management with direct control over these two safety areas.

The possibility of gaining a "more balanced" program is cited by one executive who points

out: "With limited company resources there are instances where we have to make trade-offs and compromises between work and product safety. Having both responsibilities within a single unit permits us—we hope—to obtain a more reasoned view of our priorities and responsibilities."

The combination in one unit is similarly justified, in many cases, on the basis of cost savings. For many firms, the measures needed to meet occupational health and safety requirements, along with product-safety standards, have proven to be increasingly costly. While recognizing their moral as well as statutory obligations with respect to safety, managements have become increasingly conscious of these rising costs. Some executives believe that combining these functions helps firms to keep a closer watch on such costs.

Finally, a few executives say that experience and expertise gained in one safety area have often proven useful in another. This is said to be the case, for example, with regard to the establishment of legal safeguards, requirements and procedures.

A Format to Fit the Company and Product

As noted, regardless of their own company's practices, a substantial number of the executives questioned believe that there is no inevitable "right" or "wrong" approach to the question of whether work- and product-safety assignments should be combined or separated. These executives caution that each company and product situation should be examined with an open mind. More important than anything else in arriving at an organizational decision, they say, are such determinants as the nature of the industry-product category, the regulations to which it is subject, the nature of the risks involved, and the size and diversity of company operations, staff resources, and so on. In addition, they point out that a close analysis of the extent and frequency of injury claims and safety difficulties must precede such an organizational decision.

Some executives point out that a company might logically begin with one kind of organizational pattern (e.g., a combined safety department) and then, for any number of reasons, adopt an alternative structure. Others see an "evolutionary" tendency within a combined group with the probability of "natural specialization" and growing disparity of needs between product-safety and work-safety groups.

Separation of Product-Safety and Job-Safety Responsibilities

The following are some of the reasons given by the majority of respondents who favor the separation of product-safety and job-safety responsibilities:

"We do not believe they mix well. It's like combining softball and baseball. They are similar but there are many differences."

* * *

"The two basically deal with different people and different technologies, and seem to work best as separate functions."

* * *

"There is no logic in such a combination—the functions have little or nothing in common; product safety is financial, product engineering, research and legally oriented, whereas occupational safety is people and production oriented. The fields are too large to combine and the technical backgrounds are too diverse for combination. A cooperative effort by the two departments would be more advisable."

* * *

"Occupational safety and product safety are two separate responsibilities having different goals and technologies."

* * *

"The combination of occupational and product safety violates good management concepts in a firm producing high-technology products. The content differs markedly and the required individual skills are quite different."

* * *

"It works best in our company as separate responsibilities. Quality assurance is the best vehicle for top management in product safety because it uses the network of inspection and quality control that is closest to product control."

* * *

"I feel the functions could be combined successfully in companies with a limited number of product lines. I do not, however, feel product safety can be controlled effectively by the corporate [occupational] safety department in our company due to the wide range and diversity of products we manufacture."

* * *

"Product safety deals with in-depth product design and requires professional evaluations by technical disciplines. Occupational safety is more of a line responsibility with technical assistance. The two complement each other, but should not be one."

* * *

"I do not feel that there would be any benefit to be expected from the combination of occupational and product-safety responsibilities. The two types of safety considerations are separate and barely related specialties. The occupational safety program is implemented through entirely different types of corporate functions than is the product safety program, and I not believe that a single department or position could do justice to both programs at one time."

* * *

"OSHA-type workshop problems should come under the manager of corporate facilities, a planning engineer, or, if neither is available, a manager of manufacturing. Product safety begins with design, so the chief engineer or chief chemist, or even the chief designer, should be primarily responsible. However, a single vice president might audit both programs."

* * *

"We believe these to be entirely unrelated functions, with different goals and objectives; and it would be difficult if not impossible to combine [them] into one functional responsibility, although some liaison between these functions is required."

* * *

"The two functions are significantly different and operate under different laws. The occupational safety aspect fits best with manufacturing and personnel, while product safety fits best with engineering and sales."

* * *

"The separation of responsibilities tends to focus safety efforts. But we must take care to promote frequent exchanges of ideas and expertise between the two groups."

Those Who Would Combine Work and Product Safety

A minority of the safety executives surveyed favor the combination of work-safety and product-safety responsibilities. Here are typical reasons cited:

"At the corporate level, this combination of work and product safety has many advantages. At lower levels (i.e., plant) personnel are more familiar with and involved in factors affecting them, that is, plant—OSHA and, to a lesser degree, product safety."

* * *

"It is a natural combination. However, it may require a separate unit within the department, depending on the extent of the work involved."

* * *

"The departments should be combined at the highest level of management possible. This is necessary to coordinate the diverse functional interests in a company organizational structure."

* * *

"Combining their responsibilities provides opportunities to apply to one area information and techniques developed or encountered in the other area."

* * *

"There is a relationship between the two responsibilities and an overlap of people with relevant knowledge and responsibilities which makes this combination workable."

* * *

"This is probably the best method for compliance with government regulations."

* * *

"The combination highlights all safety-related problems and channels efforts in the same direction, avoiding overlaps."

* * *

"Our corporate safety and environmental programs are broad and rigorous. Each operating division also maintains its own programs consistent with corporate efforts. We do not distinguish product safety from work safety and industrial hygiene. In our company, specific efforts on product safety relate mostly to proper packaging, labeling and transportation of these items that directly serve consumer markets."

* * *

"Starting from grass roots, a single department including occupational safety, environmental affairs, product safety, and related medical functions (toxicology, epidemiology) would be logical."

* * *

"Industrial safety and product safety are different; but since they are related, they should come under the "loss prevention" department concerned with all losses, regardless of origin."

* * *

"Combining occupational and product safety under one department head would be the most efficient design to eliminate duplication of efforts in many areas such as safety inspection, investigations and record-keeping."

Chapter 6

Responsibilities and Activities of Product-Safety Units

CERTAIN BASIC ACTIVITIES are integral to most product-safety units, whether they function on a full- or part-time basis, although their actual practices understandably differ, depending on organizational arrangements and product-safety missions. A summary of the reported activities of the product-safety units in the companies surveyed is shown in Table 8. The table represents a composite compilation of activities at various levels among divisionalized and nondivisionalized firms.

It will be recognized, however, that additional factors—particularly whether the firm's safety effort is completely centralized or completely decentralized—will affect the kinds and varieties of activities carried on by various safety units. For example, in a completely centralized arrangement, there will be no need for the corporate-level safety unit to perform any coordinating functions, since all safety responsibilities are vested with the unit. In actual practice, however, a majority of the firms studied have safety responsibilities at both a corporate and operating unit level. Therefore, it is often the inherent responsibility of the corporate level unit to coordinate and keep track of the activities of operating-level safety units.

Evaluating the Safetyworthiness of New Products

New product chronicles are replete with examples of safety failures and firms are, understandably, uncertain and concerned over the safety of the new products they introduce. This unease and concern is reflected in the responsibilities managements assign to safety units.

Product-safety executives say that there are numerous conditions that give rise to managements' worries over new products and the safety issues that may develop as a result of the introduction of these products. First, there may be uncertainty about how customers might misuse a product, or even how the product will perform under various use conditions. This makes it difficult to judge possibilities of product failure.

Often, in developing new products, a manufacturer may be working with still-uncertain design configurations, materials of construction, or manufacturing techniques that could result in hidden safety defects. For such reasons, the evaluation of the safety of new products is a common responsibility of company product-safety units, regardless of their organizational positioning. However, this activity is most likely to be assigned to units at the corporate or major division level (see Table 8).

A company's products and markets can also influence the extent to which product-safety units engage in the safety evaluation of new

Table 8: Principal Functions Performed By Product-Safety Units: All Companies[1]

Percent of Product Safety Units Performing Indicated Function

Function	In Nondivisionalized Companies	In Divisionalized Companies			
		At Corporate Level	At Group Level	At Major Division Level	At Minor Division Level
Evaluating the safetyworthiness of *new* products	87%	46%	24%	55%	41%
Investigating product-safety failures	87	46	65	30	62
Liaison with safety regulatory agencies	80	62	39	20	77
Evaluating and/or preparing product-use instructions	76	43	57	26	57
Auditing and testing the safetyworthiness of existing products	70	35	53	25	48
Setting safety performance standards for finished products	70	41	50	25	54
Evaluating patterns and trends of safety failures	67	38	43	22	51
Educating company employees in product-safety matters	67	52	49	28	65
Processing product-liability claims	65	72	33	19	85
Setting quality control standards for manufactured products	65	23	30	59	48
Setting safety standards for raw materials	63	50	53	25	42
Regulatory recordkeeping	58	33	40	19	44
Reporting safety defects to regulatory agencies	52	46	25	15	55
Planning safety education programs for products users or other outsiders	50	47	43	22	57
Managing product recall campaigns	4	3	2	1	3

[1]Based on reported practices of 242 divisionalized and 46 nondivisionalized firms, for both full- and part-time product-safety units.

products. The safety units of companies making consumer products are more likely to regard such evaluations as a major responsibility, than are their counterparts among industrial goods producers. And, comparing full-time and part-time safety units, it is found that the full-time units often report this as a major responsibility.

The actual participation of a unit in new-product evaluations can proceed in several ways. First, if a company has a new-product screening committee, a representative of the product-safety unit often serves on it. While such individuals may not have veto power over new product proposals, they do have considerable influence. A negative finding by the product-safety member reportedly will be likely to cause a new product entry to be deferred or cancelled.

Often, safety specialists' involvement with a new product begins during the development stage, at which time they confer with product design, research and development, and engineering personnel. Here, safety executives say, they are able to call on their experience with past failures (in their own company and among competitors) to influence the way in which a product is designed. For example, the safety executive for a manufacturer of small appliances says that he argued vehemently for "waterproofing" a certain new product, pointing out that despite instructions to the contrary, some consumers would be likely to immerse the appliance while cleaning it. Such an immersion could produce a fatal electrocution if the appliance was plugged in at the time. Such an accident had never taken place with one of this manufacturer's products, but the product-safety executive remembered that a competitor had encountered such difficulties.

Several executives note that they need to become involved with a product at its "concept" stage—before the designers and engineers have begun to construct prototypes. They may be able to divert efforts from certain design configurations which they consider to be inherently dangerous—for example, those that may subject users to unnecessary risks from heat, electricity, and so forth, or that may demand more skill in the product's use than logically can be expected.

The early attention of safety specialists is said to help in preventing companies from investing resources in product areas with unexceptable risk potential. "There are just too many good, safe, new product possibilities for us to be investing in," the safety executive for one consumer goods firm states. "It makes no sense to waste funds needlessly on product ventures that are likely to produce safety failures and product-liability litigation."

This manager recalls that he was instrumental some years back in persuading his company's management not to acquire a certain recreational products firm. His arguments against the acquisition proved persuasive because he was able to demonstrate the experience of other manufacturers of such products with product-liability litigation.

While new-product designers and engineers should be familiar with product-safety statutes, as well as with the dangers their product designs could pose, safety executives state that, in reality, some are not. In such instances, the safety executive can act as a consultant in determining whether a proposed new product meets relevant safety standards. The toy products division of one consumer goods firm, for example, was considering acquiring the

rights to an unusual doll that would be produced in, and imported from, the Far East. The corporate-level safety specialist, in examining the new product, found that certain parts could be easily dislodged and perhaps ingested by small children with serious consequences. The toy division's engineers found a way to redesign the doll to eliminate such parts. Such instances will become even more critical, safety managers say, as the Consumer Product Safety Commission and other regulatory bodies expand their efforts to establish safety standards for various products.

Evaluating the Safetyworthiness of Existing Products

As Table 8 also illustrates, the safety units at many different levels of the companies surveyed are expected to concern themselves with the firms' existing products as well, periodically auditing and monitoring these products. "We feel only slightly more comfortable with our existing product line than we do with newly developed products," comments the safety manager of one consumer goods manufacturer. For such reasons, safety units in many businesses continue to check on potential hazards in the use of products no longer new to the manufacturer. Products previously found to be safe may develop new uses, new classes of customers, or be affected by new materials or technologies used in their manufacture. In the process of such change, new safety hazards could develop.

A producer of disinfectant chemicals, for example, recalls that several of its standard, supposedly safe, cleaning preparations suddenly joined the "dangerous" category overnight, with the discovery that a hexachlorophene additive, used by the company for a number of years, had been declared a carcinogen suspect. Another firm, a producer of paint spray equipment, found that a standard spraying technology—utilized for many of the company's products—was allegedly capable of driving paint particles through a user's skin and producing a gangrenous infection.

In some instances, product-safety executives

say they have been instrumental in advising top management to drop or sell off certain products—or entire divisions—which seem prone to safety and product-liability problems. For example, the product-safety officers of three major companies advised—and the companies have acted on this advice—the divestiture of divisions manufacturing recreational boats. In these instances, the product-safety officers' assessment of their firms' position, vis-à-vis present and potential product-liability suits, led them to believe that such products were—for those firms—more of a casualty risk than their profit potential could justify.

During discussions with other safety executives it was found that in numerous instances companies have had good reason to rue the day that they decided to launch, or continue selling, a particular product. One chemicals and metals refiner, for example, marketed—primarily as a service to round out its product line—a particularly toxic chemical, which was used by sheep farmers to poison coyotes. Unfortunately, the farmers used excessive amounts of this poison, and several protected species of birds, primarily the golden eagle, ingested some of the poison as a result of eating contaminated or poisoned animals. The public outcry over the use of this material was said to have put the company on several public interest groups' "enemies list"; and even several years after the product had been withdrawn (at a cost that exceeded the gross sales revenue for the product) the firm continued to be the target of safety and environmental activists' attacks.

In the hope of minimizing such surprises, company managements have charged their safety units with the responsibility for focusing on existing products and accepted technologies and continuing to audit these products and technologies in search of unforeseen safety difficulties. For this purpose, a variety of audit checklists and questionnaires have been developed (see Chapter 2, for example, and the ITT form, Exhibit 18) to assist safety executives in keeping managements informed of the safety characteristics of their company's products.

From an organizational standpoint, the safety audit itself is most often conducted at the operating unit level. But the design of the audit and the compilation of data obtained from the audits, including follow-up on tardy audit reporting, is most often the duty of a central or corporate-level safety unit.

The companies studied do report some difficulties in conducting safety audits—particularly in determining precisely how customers use products. "Until we created a product safety department," one hardware producer's safety manager states, "I don't think the company had an accurate picture of exactly how our customers use our products. But an examination of the claims incidents of the past several years, as well as a second look at some of our product-liability litigation, convinced us we had better pay much more attention to the 'unconventional' uses of our products. This is an area that seems to produce an abnormally high number of claims."

The same executive goes on to point out that certain products were redesigned as a result of such analyses so as to reduce the possibilities for misuse. And, in a few cases, the company's products were withdrawn from distribution channels where unsophisticated consumers might gain access to a product demanding professional skill in its use. The firm's labeling system was also reviewed and new instructions drafted to alert customers to the dangers that might result from mishandling certain of the company's tool products.

Investigating and Analyzing Product-Safety Failures

A majority of the firms studied make the investigation and analysis of safety failures a primary responsibility of their safety units. In this connection, product-safety units are often charged with numerous investigatory responsibilities. (Exhibits 24 and 25 illustrate the work flow and investigative responsibilities as described by a major food retailer.) For example, safety specialists may be called upon to interview injury complainants in an attempt to pinpoint how product-related accidents

Exhibit 24: A Retailer's Flow Chart for Identification and Action on Product-Safety Hazards—Giant Food, Inc.

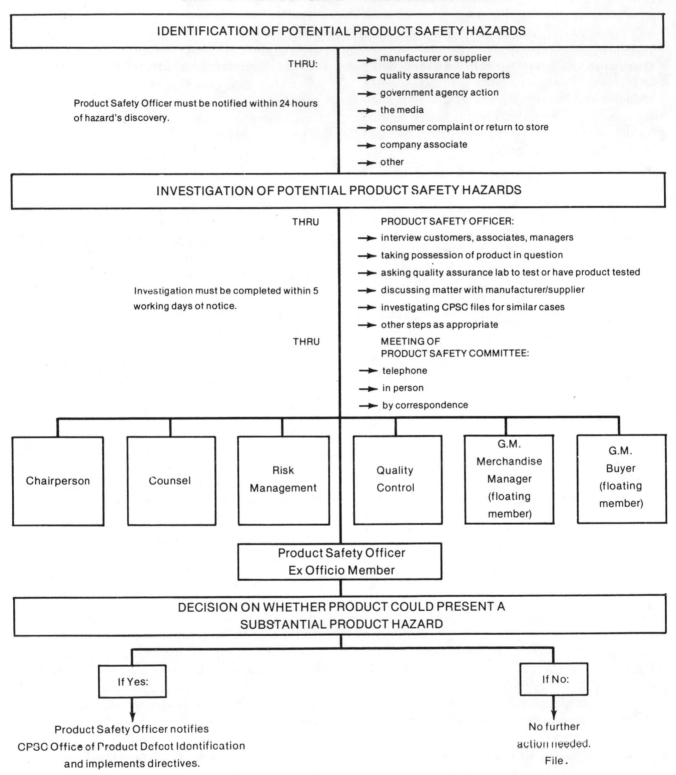

GIANT'S PRODUCT SAFETY PROGRAM OUTLINE

IDENTIFICATION OF POTENTIAL PRODUCT SAFETY HAZARDS

Product Safety Officer must be notified within 24 hours of hazard's discovery.

THRU:
- → manufacturer or supplier
- → quality assurance lab reports
- → government agency action
- → the media
- → consumer complaint or return to store
- → company associate
- → other

INVESTIGATION OF POTENTIAL PRODUCT SAFETY HAZARDS

Investigation must be completed within 5 working days of notice.

THRU
PRODUCT SAFETY OFFICER:
- → interview customers, associates, managers
- → taking possession of product in question
- → asking quality assurance lab to test or have product tested
- → discussing matter with manufacturer/supplier
- → investigating CPSC files for similar cases
- → other steps as appropriate

THRU
MEETING OF PRODUCT SAFETY COMMITTEE:
- → telephone
- → in person
- → by correspondence

| Chairperson | Counsel | Risk Management | Quality Control | G.M. Merchandise Manager (floating member) | G.M. Buyer (floating member) |

Product Safety Officer
Ex Officio Member

DECISION ON WHETHER PRODUCT COULD PRESENT A SUBSTANTIAL PRODUCT HAZARD

If Yes:

Product Safety Officer notifies CPSC Office of Product Defect Identification and implements directives.

If No:

No further action needed. File.

Exhibit 25: A Retailer's Procedures for Investigating a Product-Safety Complaint—Giant Food, Inc.

PROCEDURES FOR PRODUCT SAFETY OFFICER

Responsibility

The Product Safety Officer (PSO) is the coordinator of the Product Safety Program. PSO's responsibilities include handling the overall investigations of potential product hazards, preparing reports to be reviewed by Giant's Product Safety Committee, and communicating with the Consumer Product Safety Commission.

Steps To Be Initiated

Identification of Potential Product Safety Hazard

- A potential product safety hazard may be identified to the PSO through any of the following means:

  1　Manufacturer's or supplier's notification
  2　Giant Quality Assurance Lab Report
  3　Government agency action
  4　The media
  5　Consumer complaint or return to a store through:
  　　Phone contact
  　　Letter
  　　Trip to the store
  　　Insurance claim
  6　Company associate
  7　Other.

- Whatever the source, Giant's policy is to assure that the PSO is notified of every potential safety hazard within 24 hours of its discovery.

Investigation of Potential Product Safety Hazard

- Once the PSO has received a report of a potential product safety hazard, it is his/her duty to investigate the situation so that a full report and recommendations can be made to the Product Safety Committee (PSC).

- Any or all of the following steps should be included in the PSO's investigation as deemed appropriate:

  1. Interview customers, store employees, managers.
  2. Take possession of the product in question.
  3. Ask the Quality Assurance Lab to test the product or have it tested.
  4. Discuss the matter with the manufacturer, supplier, buyer, and merchandise manager.
  5. Investigate CPSC files for similar cases.
  6. Other steps as appropriate.

- All action taken is to be recorded on the Log of Safety Related Complaints & Action.

- PSO will convene a meeting(s)—by telephone, in person, or by correspondence—of the PRODUCT SAFETY COMMITTEE as soon as possible after receiving notification of a potential hazard.

  A meeting should be initiated if at all possible, within 5 working days, for the purpose of determining what, if any, further steps should be taken.

occurred. In some instances, they make attempts to simulate an accident, using the complainant's description of the product's use and the facilities of the firm's engineering and testing laboratories. Often, in cooperation with personnel from the company's quality-assurance departments, safety specialists will seek to isolate the causal factors (construction materials, fabrication faults, package shortcomings, or whatever) that may have contributed to failure. The range of steps taken by one manufacturer of small appliances is illustrative:

"We begin by gathering as much internal evidence as may be available. We check the lot number, date of manufacture, materials of construction, plant of origin, and so forth. If the subject of the complaint is a new product, we look back at the field-testing program conducted prior to product introduction to see whether or not there were any hints that a failure similar to the complainant's description could have taken place.

"Then, we arrange to interview the complainant, usually at home, and to obtain the defective appliance. We provide a product replacement and try to determine, during the field interview, exactly how the customer used the product. Some complaints are, of course, legal claims, and we are accompanied by our company's attorney—often with an offer to settle the complainant's claim.

"Once we have obtained physical possession of the product, we disassemble it and try to get an idea of exactly how much use the appliance received and whether it was stressed beyond normal limits. At the same time, we may try to simulate the accident using a similar model appliance. By that time we usually have a pretty good idea of how the accident occurred and whether or not a product breakdown or customer, misuse of the product was the primary culprit in the failure."

Product-safety units in several reporting firms maintain extensive safety complaint systems. The primary elements of such systems generally include:

(1) A copy of each written complaint, or a memo describing each complaint received by phone (see Exhibit 26);

(2) A complete description of the product in each case by generic and trade name, model number, date of manufacture, and so on;

(3) The date that each safety complaint was received and the date of the firm's initial response, as well as a copy of that response;

(4) Copies of all correspondence from the complainant, or his or her representatives, on the alleged product injury;

(5) A complete description of the injuries occurring, if any, as a result of the alleged product failure;

(6) A record of lawsuits and claims filed;

(7) A record of the final response and actions taken; and

(8) Copies of any notices to the press, customers or regulatory agencies concerning each product-safety incident.

In addition to this kind of investigating and reporting, it is also normal practice for safety units to prepare summary reports (often on a monthly basis) that describe the number and variety of safety hazard-related failures that have taken place during the latest time period covered by the reports.

The list of executives receiving such reports differs substantially from one company to the next. In many instances, however, distribution is limited to members of the product-safety committee—and to the executive to whom the principal product-safety executive reports. But sometimes the safety summary also goes to the company's chief executive; and in the case of one machine tool producer who experienced a rash of product-liability suits, periodic safety reports are now distributed to the company's board of directors as well.

Product-safety executives rely heavily on customer-complaint data for clues to the factors likely to be responsible for product failures. In this respect, several report that they work closely with their companies' claims and insurance investigators, as well as with company consumer-affairs specialists. At a food company, complaints about either the taste or effect

Exhibit 26: A Retailer's Product-Safety Complaint Form—Giant Food, Inc.

(THIS FORM IS TO BE FILLED OUT BY THE PRODUCT SAFETY OFFICER EVERY
TIME AN ISSUE IS BROUGHT BEFORE THE PRODUCT SAFETY COMMITTEE)

Date_____

LOG OF SAFETY-RELATED COMPLAINTS & ACTION

PRODUCTION DESCRIPTION:_____

MANUFACTURER: _____

STYLE NO: _____ CODE NO: _____ SIZE: _____

NATURE OF SAFETY-RELATED COMPLAINT: _____

_____

_____

_____

COMPLAINT RECEIVED FROM: _____

NAME OF CUSTOMER (if known): _____

ADDRESS: _____

DID CUSTOMER RECEIVE A REFUND? ☐ Yes ☐ No

ANY INJURY? ☐ Yes ☐ No

MANUFACTURER NOTIFIED BY: _____ DATE: _____

QUALITY CONTROL LABORATORY: DATE FORWARDED: _____

TEST RESULTS COMPLETED: _____

(Attach a copy of test results)

RISK MANAGEMENT NOTIFIED:_____(DATE)

IF PRODUCT WITHDRAWAL INDICATE REASON:

____ Company Withdrawal	____ Government Recall
____ Customer Complaint	____ News Report
____ Manufacturer's Notification	____ Associate's Call/Complaint
____ Lab Test Results	____ Other:_____

WHO INITIATED WITHDRAWAL?_____ DEPT: _____

COMMUNICATION FOR WITHDRAWAL
SENT TO STORES BY:

____ Telephone via Customer Communications	Date_____ Time _____
____ Consolidated Bulletin	Date_____ Time _____
____ Special Consolidated Bulletin	Date_____ Time _____

MESSAGE TO STORES: _____

_____

PRODUCT SAFETY COMMITTEE:

DATES OF MEETINGS _____ (Attach a complete record of

_____ all action, meetings,

_____ phone calls, etc.).

DECISION OF PSC: YES, Notify CPSC of NO, Not a substantial
substantial hazard product hazard.
☐ ☐

DATE COMPLETE REPORT FORWARDED TO CPSC: _____

DATE REPLY RECEIVED FROM CPSC: _____

of its products are checked as the most concrete evidence available of a possible quality-assurance lapse and a potential safety problem. Complaints, first received by the consumer affairs unit, are then referred to the company's claims department. If a safety issue is involved, insurance investigators gather data which are reviewed by the firm's product-safety specialists.

But not all of the items sold by the company are amenable to the same procedures. Its safety director reports: "One of our products is dog food. Here we have a real problem. The dogs can't talk, of course, and the problem of finding out what really caused a dog's illness—whether it's related to the dog food—continues to bedevil us."

Maintaining Liaison with Safety Regulatory Agencies

Product-safety units at varying organizational levels do tend to differ in their responsibilities for maintaining liaison with safety regulatory agencies. In general, corporate-level units and those units in which safety responsibilities are highly centralized, have a greater share of responsibility for maintaining the "official company contact" with safety regulators. However, the safety units at operating levels often maintain contact with federal and local regulators. However, the need for such liaison is often modest because of the division or operating unit's smaller scale of operations.

Keeping in touch with safety regulatory agencies takes many forms and requires a sense of diplomacy and balance. Product-safety executives do not wish to engage in activities that might cause them to be thought of as corporate lobbyists seeking a more lenient interpretation of safety regulations. Yet, it is necessary for them to confer in various ways with the staffs of regulatory agencies in order to coordinate their companies' safety efforts. The safety manager of one housewares company describes his firm's position this way:

"We keep in regular touch with the Consumer Products Safety Commission—regardless of whether or not we've had a 15-B (reportable safety hazard) incident. Safety regulations are constantly being reinterpreted, product standards are being developed and modified, and there are often times when we are at disagreement with the Commission's staff on the direction that they are taking on some safety regulations. We believe you cannot complain about a new regulation after it's promulgated if you have neglected to provide any input during the regulators' decision-making process. We don't lobby, but we do stay in touch and we do advise them of our thinking on those regulations and subject areas of direct concern to us."

Few product-safety units have representatives stationed in Washington to deal with federal regulatory agencies. Most contacts, instead, are on a long-distance basis, although safety executives will usually make an effort to attend briefing sessions held by regulatory commissions, Congressional hearings on safety issues, and so forth.

Developing and Setting Standards

Product-safety executives report that safety units most often contribute to the setting of standards in these areas:

(1) Safety performance standards for finished products;
(2) Safety standards for raw materials and components; and
(3) Safety related quality-control standards for manufacturing processes.

While there are numerous governmental and trade association groups involved in the establishment of product performance standards of one kind or another, most manufacturers also set standards of performance of their own, which are designed to reduce the possibility of injury through product failure.

As an example, the product-safety staff of a cereal company inspects the plants and laboratory facilities of its raw material suppliers, so as to assure management that these suppliers are as concerned about safety as the company itself is. But few of the product-safety units have the full responsibility for developing product-safety standards; most of them engage in a cooperative effort with product designers and quality-control specialists. Companies report that this type of activity often takes place at the operating-unit level, and less so at corporate-level units, or as an activity performed by product-safety units in highly centralized organizational structures.

An analysis of several safety incidents at a metals company showed that one of its products, although it met manufacturing specifications, was dangerously weak when used in a recreational equipment applications that a number of customers had selected. Changes in processing standards, as well as in upgrading materials themselves, increased the tensile strength of the product, thus reducing the possibility of failure and customer injury. The product-safety manager in another company notes that quality-assurance standards are normally "designed to let some defects slip through." Acknowledging that his own firm cannot expect a zero-defects performance for manufacturing, he points out that, nevertheless, there are certain products where even a few defects could produce serious safety consequences. His unit was successful in "tightening up" quality standards for these products, so as to reduce the risk of injury associated with them.

Product-Liability Claims

The organizational level at which the product-safety unit is positioned is often a determinant of whether or not it is actually concerned with the processing of product-liability claims. In general, as shown in Table 8, units in non-divisionalized companies and corporate-level safety units tend to be more directly involved in claims processing.

But such responsibilities are less likely at the operating level. This participation does not mean that a safety unit has the responsibility for the legal adjudication of the safety-related claim—particularly should such a claim evolve into a lawsuit—but rather that the product-safety units provide direct help in validating claims, assessing the degree of personal or economic injury, and in communicating with claimants (see Exhibit 27).

Problems at the Consumer Product Safety Commission

According to the safety professionals surveyed, one of the most difficult regulatory agencies that they must deal with is the Consumer Product Safety Commission. In the main, the criticisms seem directed not so much at the vigor of the CPSC's regulatory efforts, but at its professional competence, organization and sense of priorities—complaints that have also been echoed by some congressional critics.[1] Among some of the comments offered by the survey respondents are the following:

- "There is so much internal bickering that we (industry) seldom seem to know who's in charge or what they really want accomplished."

—A toy manufacturer.

- "No one seems to stay around at the agency long enough to gain the product knowledge and technical expertise necessary to understand the products that the CPSC is supposed to be regulating."

—A bicycle producer.

- "The CPSC's sense of priorities isn't in touch with reality. They'll spend years developing a swimming pool slide standard, while thousands of people are being injured by dozens of other products that are more hazardous and in more widespread use."

—A housewares manufacturer.

- "No one at the agency seems at all concerned with the cost-benefits question of product modification. Some of the changes they want will price our products out of the world market."

—A sporting goods manufacturer.

[1] The Conference Board's upcoming study, *Business Perceptions of Regulatory Forms*, also focuses on such issues.

(1) Issuance, under the signature of the chief executive, of company policy pertaining to product liability.

(2) Designation of an individual, representing a top level of management, as the coordinator of product liability loss control activities.

(3) Establishing clear lines of communications so that the coordinator can successfully work with other functions and divisions within the company to achieve policy goals.

(4) Establishment of a unit loss control committee, consisting of management representatives. In the selection of the committee, consideration should be given to including personnel from research, design, engineering, legal, production, quality control, purchasing, marketing, insurance, safety and service departments.

(5) Making available to the control committee all available knowledge concerning product loss trends, past and present, to include information relating to warranty and guarantee claims, product incidents, and actual claims.

(6) Assuring that federal, state and local codes and regulations which apply to product safety are thoroughly understood and considered at appropriate operating levels and are used as <u>minimum</u> requirements in product design.

(7) Establishment of procedures for evaluation, by both research and design departments, of potential for personal injury or property damage during use, or reasonably expected misuse, of proposed new products, or changes in existing products, the result of which would be the building into products of an adequate safety level.

(8) Having final design specifications for all new products and revisions in existing products reviewed by qualified personnel.

(9) Submission of new products for further approval by nationally recognized testing agencies, when appropriate.

(10) Developing a clearly understood procedure whereby products with removable guards or safety devices <u>are</u> <u>not</u> <u>sold</u> <u>unless</u> a clear stipulation can be obtained from the customer or user that they are not desired.

(11) Arranging for the review of existing quality control procedures and their reinforcement in relation to developing product liability trends.

(12) Establishing procedures whereby all changes in production methods and techniques are reviewed from a product safety standpoint prior to their actual implementation.

(13) Insisting that critical components of a product are coded as to production place and date for easy tracing.

(14) Assuring that capacity ratings are displayed in a conspicuous and permanent manner on those products where such information is necessary.

(15) Informing suppliers of the final use of their materials or components and encouraging their suggestions regarding changes and/or improvements.

(16) Arranging for coding of components when two or more suppliers are providing identical materials or when suppliers of components are changed so that the materials can be traced.

(17) Advising field personnel regarding product liability claims and establishing a method of relaying information which becomes known to field personnel concerning possible hazards involved with a product or possible misuse of a product.

(18) Establishing a specific procedure for the investigation of all possible product liability incidents, whether received from a customer, a field service representative, a distributor, a dealer, or any other source.

(19) Arranging to have all advertising literature, brochures and labels reviewed by engineering and legal departments for accuracy so that any exaggerated performance claims can be deleted prior to release.

(20) Providing for the use of clear, complete, conspicuous and durable precautionary instructions and warning labels when a product involves inherent hazards which cannot be eliminated through design changes and/or mechanical guarding.

(21) Providing for the review of all operating and maintenance manuals by legal and engineering personnel for adequacy and accuracy prior to release.

(22) Arranging for legal counsel to review all product warranties, guarantees, clauses and disclaimers.

(23) Assuring that packaging and shipping procedures are adequate to minimize the possibility of increasing product liability loss potential during the shipment of the product.

(24) Maintaining records, through the expected life of the product, to include research, design, test, production, quality control, sales and service data.

(25) Maintain accurate product distribution lists so that if a product recall becomes necessary, it can be accomplished quickly.

(26) Providing for continual audit of all product loss control measures by the coordinator so the revisions can be quickly implemented to reflect changing trends.

The more recently formed units tend to be more actively involved in liability issues than are older units. Several of the executives say that they are currently becoming more and more active in product-liability matters and are required to spend a greater amount of their time on such issues.

Company legal departments have also come to recognize that safety units are an invaluable source of data, as well as technical assistance, in defending firms against liability claims. In several of the companies studied, the legal department has proved a valuable ally in assisting product-safety executives to gain additional staff and budgetary support.

Product-Safety Education Programs

Safety-awareness programs, conducted inside their companies, are seen by a majority of the executives surveyed as one of the principal hopes for overcoming safety problems. Several companies have developed intensive education programs to acquaint everyone—management and workers—with the need for increased product safety and the economic consequences of safety lapses. The product-safety director of a sporting goods company, for example, attends 30 to 40 sessions each year, giving presentations on the product-safety hazards he has encountered and reviewing past safety failures of the company. In addition, members of the product-safety staff of this firm meet with groups of production workers, field sales representatives, service people, and others in a continuing effort to alert them to the costs of poorly designed, manufactured or serviced products. This effort is further bolstered by bulletin board posters, leaflets and safety-orientation films shown to new employees.

The safety director does not regard this as a one-time program. "I wish that we could do this program just once and get it over with," he says. "But it seems to be a matter of educating and reeducating and I'm not sure that we will ever reach a level where we can confidently say that everyone knows about product safety and will perform accordingly."

Among other things, the educational programs of some firms include efforts to teach employees "what they can say" about the company's products. At a metals company, this has led to the successful change of a long-standing practice that had salesmen making certain technical recommendations to their customers. When a customer would inquire as to the kind and strength of a product required for a particular application, a salesman, who had been trained to provide such recommendations, would then suggest a particular grade.

But, in time, difficulties arose when a few customers launched product-liability suits in which they claimed that they had relied on the company's salesman for counsel on the correct type of metal, and alleged that it was the producer's fault when the customer's product failed—regardless of the misapplication of the metal raw material. On advice of the company's product-safety manager, the salesmen were instructed to refrain from making specific recommendations about the type of company product that a customer should use in specific cases. Instead, the salesmen provide a customer with a list of material specifications, leaving it to the customer to decide which grade is best for the intended application.

One concern of many safety managers is that in the minds of the companies' employees the product too often becomes entirely divorced from its uses and users. Thus, some education programs make a deliberate attempt to have certain employees "get to know" the uses and users of the products for which they are responsibile. One of the best ways, one toiletry company spokesman says, is to encourage employees and their families themselves to make use of the company's products. The executive claims that employees are then more likely to be sensitive to the potential injury that can result from product failures.

In some instances, a company's safety-education program actually promotes the discouragement of a product's purchase by certain prospects. There are products, for example, made by one chemical company that are so hazardous that the firm's product-safety department monitors their distribution and advises the sales department on whether prospective new customers are qualified to receive such materials. Ordinarily, the sale of these research chemicals is limited to no more than a few dozen laboratories known to have the safety standards and equipment capable of handling them.

While this represents extreme safety-unit involvement in customer selection, other product-safety units reportedly discourage their company's marketers from promoting products to classes of customers known to be litigation-prone or frequently careless in their use of products. This intervention may take such forms as suggesting that products not be advertised in certain media or that minimum purchase quantities be large enough to discourage amateur or inexperienced users from purchasing these materials.

Regulatory Reporting and Recordkeeping

Somewhat less than half of the product-safety units studied at various organizational levels are at least partially responsible for maintaining safety records, as required by various regulatory agencies, as well as reporting to these agencies on imminent product-safety hazards. In general, consumer goods producers, and firms with long-established safety units, give this responsibility to their safety units more often than do other types of manufacturers.

The provisions of the Consumer Product Safety Act (e.g., Section 15-B), the Food Drug and Cosmetic Act, and similar federal safety statutes, require that companies subject to these laws keep records of product-safety failures and report such failures to the appropriate regulatory bodies. Moreover, there are civil and criminal sanctions applicable to those firms that neglect to maintain such records or fail to provide notice to regulators of imminent safety hazards.

It might seem that the head of the product-safety unit would be the most logical individual to be vested with such responsibilities. Yet, several companies, while expecting that safety units will naturally keep close tabs on safety miscues, nevertheless assign to others the responsibility to report safety failures officially.

One company's spokesman explains its reasons for following this approach:

"The statutory requirements of these acts [product safety statutes] demand that once a responsible individual in charge of reporting becomes apprised of a safety incident, he or she report it to a regulatory agency within a matter of hours—or days at the most. But often, our investigation of a suspicious event—one that could or could not indicate an imminent safety hazard—may take several days to conclude. In order to be legally in conformance with the act—and there is some question in my mind about the legality—we try to insulate the executive charged with reporting the incident from knowledge of the incident until we have concluded the first stage of an internal investigation.

"Since the product-safety department is the unit performing the investigation, we believe its director should not also be responsible for reporting these cases—since the director becomes apprised of the difficulties while we are still in the 'suspicion stage' and would be duty-bound to report the incident to regulators. Many of the safety failures we encounter never get beyond the suspicion stage. They are not actually safety 'hazards' and we feel we would be overreporting if we had to file on each and every such case."

Company and product-safety situations do differ, of course, but there could be real dangers in the approach just described. The Consumer Product Safety Commission recently clamped down on Section 15-B reporting delays, fining a housewares company $385,000, and a sporting goods firm $125,000, for failing to report promptly product hazards brought to their attention by consumer complaints. And a revision of the 15-B rule states that a company is presumed to have "substantial hazard" information if *any* official or employee of the company has received such information.

Managing Product Recalls

While a product recall is certainly a critical activity related to safety, only a small number of the product-safety units has the overall responsibility for "managing" such campaigns. Their role is rather one of providing advice, monitoring recall effectiveness, consulting with regulatory agencies, and the like. A recall campaign itself is most often directly managed by either a quality-assurance or marketing executive, often with assistance from the company's legal and public relations staffs. The logic behind such an arrangement is that line officers most often have the logistics available to them—and the authority—to administer a large-scale product recall effectively. They can command the resources necessary to accomplish such a task.

Product-safety executives are vitally concerned with the results of their companies' recall campaigns. Sometimes, recall decisions have to be made independently of the advice of federal regulatory agencies—simply because the economic consequences of not recalling the product may be grave, regardless of the company's position with regard to adherence to a safety statute.

For example, a retail firm received 28 complaints of bicycles breaking as a result of metal fatigue in the front fork. This was reported to the CPSA, but the agency did not believe it necessary to initiate a major recall. Despite that advice, the company decided, for its own benefit, that it would probably be better to get back the additional 140,000 bikes that might have been affected by such a defect—and so a major product recall was begun.

Safety-defective products that are not returned are often said to be "time bombs" and capable of producing injuries and product-liability litigation at any time. For this reason, product-safety professionals, as well as their counterparts in the companies' legal departments, are increasingly concerned over the efficiency of product-recall campaigns; and

safety executives say that they are becoming more involved in the operation of such campaigns—despite the fact they do not have assigned responsibility to manage such efforts.

Current evidence suggests that there has been no diminution in the number of product recalls experienced by the American economy. In the automotive sector, a bellwether area for recall, more than 60 million cars have been recalled—equivalent to nearly half of the nation's 140 million registered vehicles. It is estimated by the National Highway Traffic Safety Administration that nearly 12 million may have been recalled in one recent year alone.

New-Product Hazards

Several safety executives point to the danger that new-product promoters, in their haste to get new entries to the market, may sometimes overlook product features that could result in safety problems later on. Among others, the Minnesota Mining and Manufacturing Company attempts to overcome this difficulty by requiring division managers to have a completed pre-market checklist for each new product they propose to market. The company's program, and its anticipated benefits, are shown in Exhibit 28.

Product-Safety Job Descriptions

Many companies still do not have job descriptions for the executives in charge of product safety. In some instances, as noted earlier, safety responsibilities have been appended to an existing job description. But, for the most part, such addenda tend to be brief and of a generalized nature.

However, several of the firms studied have drafted job descriptions for their safety executives; and the model job description, and the examples shown in the pages that follow, are illustrative of these efforts.

Exhibit 28: Description of New-Product-Safety Guidelines—3M Company

THE PROGRAM

The procedures suggested in this brochure on planned product responsibility draw from the product development processes of many successful 3M divisions. These processes have managed to solve or eliminate delays by detecting weak spots early...and by anticipating obstacles.

Basically, the program suggests getting fundamental knowledge first, evaluating it, then deciding whether or not to continue. Responsibilities for each task are directed to an individual, with the "team" working together for strategy and for making recommendations. As the work progresses, the bank of knowledge grows so that decisions are based on sound judgment.

The program, however, is not a code of laws. Custom tailoring is encouraged to fit the specific needs of a division or department. These are guidelines so that when the product is ready for sale, the criteria for product responsibility will have been met. These guidelines are intended to assist in the process of new or modified product introduction once the innovator's idea has solidified sufficiently to require formal approval to move toward the commercial development of the product.

Advance approval of the Marketing Policy Committee (and, therefore, adherence to product responsibility guidelines) is required before any new or significantly modified product is sold. A new product is defined as any product, raw material, semi-finished product, process or equipment being offered for sale for the first time. A significantly modified product is one which represents a change in a present product offering patentable opportunities or having legal or ethical impact on corporate responsibility. It is also suggested the same consideration be given to established products entering new markets; e.g., an industrial-consumer product being sold to the home consumer.

BENEFITS

Advantages of this long-range product development process are many:
. it provides a competitive sales advantage for the sales force...documented evidence of reliable, safe, quality products;
. it compresses the time needed to bring a product to commercialization by providing an orderly process for management review and decision making...and by suggesting the time-saving assistance of staff resource groups;
. it reduces risk and increases profit potential. Products that are going to make it surface quickly so that time and money investments are secure;
. it identifies the factors essential to the development of products and limits straying off or emphasizing areas of lesser consequence;
. it expands personal competencies and knowledge through contact with experienced professionals in specialized areas of development;
. it assures investigation into areas of product responsibility and guarantees compliance with corporate policy.

The 3M Company is committed to produce useful goods and services that are safe, reliable, environmentally acceptable, of consistent quality, and to represent them truthfully in sales, advertising, packaging, and sales promotion.

The Product Safety Manager will function as follows:

1. Develop data from all operating divisions relative to product loss control. This information will serve to point out the areas in which corrections are needed. These data should include but not be limited to:

   a. Product safety hazard analysis.

   b. Loss trends.

   c. Warranty or guaranty claims.

   d. Product incidents and claim history; i.e., malfunctions, failures, accidents, misuse.

   e. Production volume, sales volume, distribution and use data as needed to accurately define the extent of possible future liability.

   f. Complete the information loop to designers to benefit from exposure experience.

   g. Provide safety inputs into product labeling, warnings and use instructions.

   h. Incorporate safety procedures in all installation, repair and final disposal of product.

   i. To coordinate those functions to determine if they comply with the company product safety policy.

2. Keep abreast of all federal, state, and local laws, codes and regulations applicable to product safety. Disseminate to involved individuals information that will aid in complying with the appropriate legislation.

3. Review quality assurance and control, and safety procedures, specifications, test records, and sampling plans to make sure that accurate safeguards are being exercised at all operating levels (a) for compliance of the product with existing quality and safety standards, and, (b) for shipment of only those products which comply with these standards.

4. Conduct audits as needed of operating procedures and records relative to product safety and loss control, determine the effectiveness of such procedures and the adequacy of these records, and communicate data to management in order to expand or improve these procedures.

5. Disseminate appropriate information from the Product Safety and Loss Control Committee to the operating division managers, so that requirements, guidelines, and criteria are fully understood and available.

6. Maintain membership and participation in appropriate outside organizations such as trade and professional associations, consumer-related groups, governmental and quasi-governmental agencies, and similar groups to keep abreast of new requirements during their development. This includes monitoring of, and participation in the activities of standards-generating organizations and other selected end-product-oriented technical societies. This will include corporatewide coordination to assure a unified company attitude on resulting standards.

7. Encourage and stimulate a free flow of communication among corporate, division, supervisory, and technical branches of the Company in all matters of product safety and loss prevention. In support of this, a library and repository of information will be established, and its contents made available to, or its information circulated to all involved parties. This will not abrogate the responsibility of division operating management to remain informed of latest developments through their independent sources.

8. Organize and coordinate training so that all operating managements and other involved individuals become knowledgeable in the required safeguards. Special training will also be given to sales, customer relations, customer service, and other personnel who deal directly with purchasers or users, stressing the proper manner of communication of product safety information.

9. As chairman of the Product Safety and Loss Control Committee, the manager is to provide all of the above information to the Committee.

[1]Model job description as provided by the National Safety Council, Chicago, Illinois and reprinted with their permission.

Exhibit 30: Job Description, Corporate Director of Quality Assurance, Environmental Control and Occupational Safety—Acme Corporation[1]

Basic Function:

This position is under the general guidance of the Vice President, Administration, and is responsible for corporate direction of the product quality assurance system, employee safety, and environmental control at operating facilities.

Reporting to this position are the Manager of Environmental Control, the Division Quality Assurance Managers.

Nature and Scope:

The Quality Assurance responsibility for product safety includes the responsibilities for a total product quality system including the need to make certain that all products and facilities are in regulatory compliance. Through the Division Quality Assurance Managers, the Director is responsible for direction of the USA products quality assurance programs. The principal effort for the divisions is to provide quality activities which assure adherence to established quality standards with resulting direct impact on operational costs and profits. The Director is to develop, recommend, and actively seek commitment to corporate quality policy and product quality assurance systems from operations and plant managers on a continuing basis to assure compliance with quality standards and regulatory requirements.

The Director is responsible for the Corporate Quality Assurance Policy and Procedure Manuals and revisions covering vendor audits, approval of vendors of sensitive materials, good manufacturing practices (GMP's), sensitive material purchasing, and other specific directions as needed to provide total Quality Assurance systems.

The Director is responsible for an audit of products and facilities and a report to management of his findings. This includes an evaluation of any significant division quality, pollution, or employee safety problem and follow-up of corrective actions by others. The ultimate action may be to shut down any facility that is operating in such a way.

The Director works with government and industry groups to develop areas of interest which are of mutual benefit to the industry and the consumer.

Technical advice is provided to divisions and plants on a wide variety of regulatory compliance matters. Advice and counsel are given on capital appropriations relating to facility expenditures to comply with business needs and compliance. Planned facilities are reviewed from a regulatory compliance viewpoint.

By directions to the Manager of Environmental Control, appropriate pollution control solutions are achieved for corporate problems. Contact with government and industry associations is maintained for knowledge of regulations on air, water, noise, and solid waste and interpretation for action programs at facilities. Recommendations are made to management for correction of environmental problems, including anticipated capital expenditures.

In the area of employee safety, the Director encourages, and coordinates the divisions to achieve good safety performance. Occupational Safety and Health Act (OSHA) procedures and regulations are communicated to operating units. Safety deficiencies are identified by facility audits, and appropriate capital projects to achieve OSHA compliance are reviewed. Reporting of safety results is provided to management and surveillance is maintained for mandatory OSHA reporting. Efforts are made through standards-setting organizations to direct future regulations.

The Director is responsible for appropriate contacts to other corporate staff departments, divisions, and subsidiaries on product quality matters, and follow-up corrective activity on facility-related problems, through corporate law, corporate insurance, technical research, and to integrate the total effort by effective coordination.

The Director is to give advice and counsel to corporate management on matters pertaining to product quality and safety, pollution control, and employee safety.

The Director has the responsibility to recommend any needed policy or program changes and the budget required to accomplish the results agreed to by the management process contract.

1/ Actual company name withheld at firm's request. Description modified to eliminate company, division or product references.

BASIC FUNCTION:

Assures that the programs and procedures necessary to detect, confirm and correct potential product safety problems, to assure customer protection in compliance with Company policy and applicable laws and regulations, are developed and maintained.

PRINCIPAL RESPONSIBILITIES AND DUTIES:

1. Assures the development and maintenance of comprehensive system to evaluate the nature and extent of potential product problems and initiate the action required to effectively resolve the problem... including:

    a)   Formalized Product Safety Action System.
    b)   Monitors trends in development of Product Safety standards and regulations.
    c)   Assists the Legal Department in its contracts with all relevant commissions, agencies and bureaus on our Company's position relative to product safety standards and/or regulations - including hearings held by the Consumer Product Safety Commission.
    d)   Maintains a centralized Company reference file of information generated from both the U.S. Government and consumer groups pertaining to safety matters.
    e)   Provides the buying departments, branch buying offices, foreign buying offices, merchandise testing center, quality control department, consumer affairs, public relations departments with up-to-date pertinent information regarding the development of safety standards and other safety regulations.
    f)   Develops, in conjunction with the Legal Department, policies and procedures for the retrieval and retention of customer identification information on appropriate lines of merchandise.
    g)   Develops and coordinates, in conjunction with the Buying Departments, programs for supplier education on product safety matters.

2. Visits regional and district offices, stores, catalog desks, service centers, and catalog distribution centers to obtain first-hand information of effectiveness of safety programs.

3. Information and statistics for Consumer Product Safety Commission of corrective actions taken.

4. Recommendations for establishing the Company's position on product safety matters.

5. Establishment of the field investigation, responsibility, action and report network.

Exhibit 32: Charter and Role of Product-Safety and Reliability Division— A Metals Manufacturer[1]

CHARTER AND ROLE

The Product Safety and Reliability Division is accountable for assuring that the designs and products of the Company and its subsidiaries are produced and delivered to customers in conformance with the emerging doctrine of strict product liability and in compliance with government legislation. This includes:

1. Assuring that product safety and reliability policy is developed, communicated and observed by the Company profit centers and subsidiaries.

2. Interpretation and communication of legislation pertinent to product safety and reliability.

3. Advising regarding standards and procedures for design, development, manufacturing and quality control, consistent with the degree of risk for each product sold or proposed for sale.

4. Recommending procedures for furnishing relevant data to customers and handling customer complaints.

5. Evaluating and assuring consistent and accurate representation of warranties, disclaimer statements, advertisements and other promotional materials.

6. Monitoring overall company performance, informing top management of results and recommending suggestions for improvement.

1/ Company name withheld at firm's request.

Exhibit 33: Charter Statement, Environmental Safety and Technical Information Group—An Oil Company

SCOPE

ESTIG is responsible for the ESTIG function worldwide, excluding those ESTIG activities assigned to other units by the Chief Executive Officer.

DEFINITIONS

Functional Responsibility - The establishment and maintenance of policies and procedures for the conduct of the ESTIG function.

Administrative Responsibility - Direct authority over the performance and direction of assigned ESTIG functions.

DUTIES

(A)   General Assignments

   (1)   Act as corporate management's agent in all ESTIG matters throughout the corporation.

   (2)   Advise and recommend to management --

- providing informational research and analysis as necessary;

- anticipating trends in ESTIG needs and applications;

- recommending to corporate and operating management appropriate positions on ESTIG-related events, concepts or conditions.

   (3)   Develop and maintain ESTIG proficiency --

- maintaining awareness of current ESTIG developments, techniques, skills, equipment, systems, etc.;

- initiating or participating with others in the planning, development and implementation of new or improved ESTIG methods or systems.

   (4)   Perform ESTIG function planning --

- projecting the impact of planned corporate and operating management's growth and expansion on future ESTIG requirements;

- determining the availability and providing, at time of need, the skills and capacity to fill the projected requirements.

B.   Specific Assignments - The Environmental Safety and Technical Information Group (ESTIG) has functional and administrative responsibility for:

   (1)   Accumulating, maintaining and disseminating data pertaining to safety and health information as well as regulatory status for all products and materials handled by the company.

- identify corporate exposure to legal requirements promulgated by government agencies to regulate such products and materials.

(2) Determining if products or commodities meet any of the criteria for hazardous materials as published by various governmental agencies and disseminating the positive results of these determinations to appropriate departments.

(3) Providing, for the corporation, special safety and health statements required for inclusion on product labels.

(4) Registering regulated products, materials and producing and using plants, as required by government regulations.

(5) Arranging for laboratory testing and analysis (principally toxicological and health hazard) to determine potential hazards involved in the use of raw materials and chemicals.

(6) Providing technical assistance to customers on hazardous properties and regulated status of the company's products.

(7) Reviewing technical information documents prior to general distribution for accuracy of information pertaining to the hazardous nature and regulatory status of products or materials.

(8) Assessing the work area environment --

   . develop and conduct monitoring and employee surveillance programs relative to hazardous and toxic materials, noise, heat stress, etc.;

   . monitor ambient air beyond plant perimeters, where necessary, for presence of hazardous and/or toxic materials above acceptable limits;

   . recommend personnel protective equipment for those areas where potential exposure to toxic and/or hazardous materials exists;

      – work with engineering to develop appropriate modifications of equipment and processes to eliminate or mitigate adverse health and physiological conditions,

      – work with the Corporate Medical Officer in developing the necessary medical compliance procedures and employee health surveillance programs.

9 Developing and conducting programs to educate and train employees in the aspects of industrial hygiene.

Chapter 7

The Product-Safety Audit

WITHOUT a special study of the situation, company safety executives say, it is often as difficult to determine the condition of a firm's product-safety preparedness as it is to assess its financial condition without a careful examination of the company's records. For this reason, occasional reliance on a formal product-safety audit has gained in popularity among a number of companies studied. While still a minority practice, the procedure is judged by adherents to be of significant importance as one of the best hopes for establishing the safetyworthiness of existing and future products.

The primary intent of such audits is: (1) to determine whether various divisions or operations are conforming to established standards for product safety; and (2) to uncover new areas of concern, areas in which established company products or practices—regardless of the fact they may meet existing safety standards—may nonetheless pose potential safety hazards.

A safety audit is generally carried out by product-safety professionals from within the firm. (Relatively few companies report the use of consultants for such services.) Occasionally, a task force with representatives from other functional areas as well will be commissioned to conduct the audit, and at times other specialists—such as the firm's legal counsel—

may be asked to perform it. In multidivisional firms, an audit at the division level is sometimes the responsibility of the general manager of the division who, in turn, often delegates such responsibility—where no formal product-safety responsibilities have already been established—to the divisional quality assurance or engineering manager.

A safety audit may take anywhere from one month to a year or more to complete, depending on the scope and circumstances of the task. A primary aim usually is to analyze the company's vulnerability to product-safety mishaps and to product-liability litigation. To accomplish this, the audit often focuses on two areas. The first is the so-called "pre-sale" checkout; during this phase, the auditors are likely to examine practices and controls involving such things as product design; adherence to design specifications; product reliability; manufacturing standards; and the inspection and testing of materials and finished products. They may also scrutinize, for potential safety liabilities, the company's advertising efforts; the ways in which the products are packaged; the instructional materials provided to product users; and training given to sales and service personnel relating to product demonstration and use.

A second phase of the audit focuses on the firm's likely liabilities *after* products have been sold, particularly on product servicing; standby procedures for product recall; and on how products might be modified in the field or misused by customers.

Planning the Safety Audit

Unlike most other kinds of internal audits—such as financial and other functional reviews, company adherence to equal employment opportunity goals, and the like—product-safety audits cover a broad range of company activities. They cover from product design and testing in engineering and research and development functions, to post-sales service, as measured by sales and service personnel. Among other things, company executives say, such audits usually require a more detailed review of how the company's products are being designed, manufactured and distributed. "You think you know what your company is making and selling, and how it's brought to the marketplace," one safety professional says. "But when you begin a safety audit you soon discover that there are many things about your company's products and markets that you did not know about. It's a good idea to ground yourself in product lore and distribution know-how before you begin a formal audit effort."

Often, to accomplish such a goal, a series of meetings are held with key personnel in order to become acquainted with recent changes in companies' product mix, sales and distribution practices, and so forth. Then, auditors frequently prepare an audit checklist. Some use a master checklist in auditing the safety situation in various operating divisions. But all point out that the checklist is primarily a starting point, a reminder of the principal areas of concern—that is, design, quality assurance, the ways in which claims are handled, and so forth. As would be expected, safety executives point out, the product-safety needs of nearly every operating unit are unique and no general checklist will fully satisfy the requirements of a unit.

The discussion that follows includes details on some of the questions most frequently addressed in product-safety audits.

Product Design

One worry, frequently, is whether personnel involved in the design of a company's products have a firm, realistic view of who the ultimate users of the products are likely to be and the ways in which they are likely to use—or, possibly, misuse—them. (One firm's admonitions to product designers is shown in Exhibit 25.)

The design audit may seek to determine just how familiar product designers are with the users—as well as with the products they are responsible for. Safety executives say that consumer expectations about product performance are often built up as a result of exposure to advertising (particularly television advertising, which demonstrates the product or like products in use), as well as by descriptions that appear on packaging, claims made by salesmen, and so forth. As a result of such exposures, consumers build up anticipations about how products will perform and how they are to be employed.

As an example, a housewife may observe that certain small appliances can be immersed for cleaning purposes. This develops an expectation that small electrical appliances of this type can be safely immersed in water. But a product designer may have no intention of making a product with such moisture resistance. Thus, customer expectations about how a product is to be used, or how it will perform, may well turn out to be at odds with the designer's expectations. Design audits do help to reconcile such views. But, most importantly, the design audit also seeks to confirm that product designers are fully aware of, and their efforts are in accordance with, federal, state and local safety statutes as they apply to the characteristics of products (e.g., voltage, wiring capacity, use limitations, and so forth). Typical questions posed during the design audit are likely to be:

(1) Who is the ultimate customer for this product—taking into account age, sex, income, physical aptitude and characteristics, familiarity

and experience with such products and how they are used, mechanical aptitudes, and so forth?

(2) What are the primary functions that the company expects this product to perform?

(3) How do the firm's product-performance levels meet or exceed consumers' expectations for the products?

(4) What existing federal, state, local or industry standards apply to this product's design, manufacture, distribution and ultimate use?

(5) What new or pending standards or legislation may apply to the product?

(6) What experience has the company or its competitors had with like products or designs as far as accidents, claims and litigation are concerned? Are product designers fully familiar with how the product may be misused and the subsequent consequences of such misuse?

(7) Do product designs incorporate all those safety features (e.g., interlocks, guards and similar safeguard provisions) that are appropriate for a product of this type and for its intended or conceivable range of use?

(8) Are necessary warnings concerning operating hazards, dangers of misuse, and so on permanently affixed to the product?

(9) Have unnecessary design hazards (such as sharp points, rough machine edges, heat or electrical exposure hazards, etc.), been eliminated?

(10) Has the product been designed with ease of servicing in mind—particularly with regard to those service factors that impinge in some manner on a product's safety performance?

(11) Has the product been tested under extreme conditions of usage (high voltage, temperature variations, vibration conditions, and so forth)?

(12) Have competitor products of the same type been analyzed to determine whether or not they offer safety advantages the company's products do not?

(13) Are there inherent weaknesses in any of the materials of construction used to fabricate the product; and how might such weaknesses be reflected in product failure?

(14) Have reliability standards been established for the product, and does this design meet or exceed these standards?

(15) Does the product, by its design, in any way pose potential long-range hazards to the environment?

(16) Does the product design impose unreasonably restrictive manufacturing specifications which could, in turn, result in manufacturing quality assurance problems? Is it reasonable to believe that this design can be produced in volume without quality difficulties?

(17) Does the product design take into account problems that might arise in shipping or storage (such as product degradation, breakage, etc.), that could pose safety hazards?

(18) Have the product designers prepared technical recommendations on how the product is best used, maintained, serviced, labeled and packaged?

(19) Have the planned product-instruction materials been fully tested and evaluated (including the need for bilingual instructions where desirable)?

Manufacturing

How a product is manufactured can affect the kinds of things that can go wrong with a product, increasing the likelihood that it will prove unsafe to users. Safety executives conducting a manufacturing audit are especially concerned that production personnel have an appreciation of the consequences of manufacturing faults relating to product failure. In addition, they want to be able to appraise how satisfactory are the communications mechanisms between manufacturing and other functional groups concerned with safety—for example, engineering, quality assurance, design and marketing. Examples of questions that may be asked regarding manufacturing operations in a safety audit are the following:

(1) Does the manufacturing department have available and understand all the approved design drawings and specifications for the product?

(2) Do manufacturing personnel know applicable safety standards, and understand them as they apply to product manufacturing?

(3) Are effective communications links maintained with design and engineering specialists, allowing production personnel to alert such specialists to difficulties encountered in meeting design specifications for the product?

(4) Is there a system for rating various raw material and component suppliers on their conformance to component specifications?

(5) Are substitutions of materials and components made only with the knowledge and approval of appropriate personnel in the design, engineering or quality-assurance units?

(6) Are in-process design changes instituted in such a way as to minimize the introduction of new safety hazards?

(7) Is there an adequate record kept of raw material and component relationships so as to identify codes for finished products?

(8) Are existing manufacturing facilities and experience equal to the task of meeting product-design specifications—particularly as they apply to safety-related product features?

(9) Does the work-planning and scheduling process of the manufacturing department take into account product-safety requirements?

(10) Is there an effective orientation program for production personnel to acquaint them with the importance of product-safety vigilance and the consequences of manufacturing failures affecting the safety of the firm's products?

(11) How are raw materials, components and finished product assemblies that do not conform with safety specifications dealt with (e.g., reworked, scrapped, etc.)?

(12) If the company has rework stations, what is the percentage of output that originates there; and how can dependence on these rework stations be minimized?

Quality Assurance

Playing a pivotal role in product safety, of course, is the inspection force that assures continuing adherence to design and manufacturing specifications and removal of nonconforming products from the marketplace.

Naturally, quality-assurance specialists recognize the relationship between quality-assurance practices and product safety. But these specialists also have a substantial degree of latitude—and safety executives endorse such discretion—in deciding whether "borderline" products (those that are only slightly off specifications) should be permitted to be sold. Obviously, safety auditors want to make certain that quality-assurance personnel are using such discretion wisely. In addition, they want answers to such basic questions as:

(1) Have complete quality-control specifications been established for all raw materials, components and manufacturing techniques used in the product's production?

(2) Have finished-product specifications, which take into account usage under adverse conditions, been similarly established?

(3) Are all raw materials, components and finished products adequately identified by lot or serial number?

(4) Is there an adequate line of communication to engineering, design and marketing personnel—for alerting them to quality lapses?

(5) Is there an adequate recordkeeping system to document the procedures employed in the production of products which might later be found to be quality defective?

(6) Have mock product recalls been conducted in order to determine the feasiblity of identifying products already shipped, and to assay the difficulties encountered in recovering such products?

(7) Are quality-assurance personnel fully conversant with applicable specifications—federal, state or industry—relating to product safety?

(8) Is there a system for recovering from the sales force, component parts or raw materials from all safety-defective products so that they

may be analyzed to pinpoint exactly the causes of failure?

(9) Does the quality-assurance department regularly review all instructions that materials resellers and users of the product receive to determine whether the information poses potential safety difficulties?

Marketing

Members of the company's marketing department often provide the stimulus for a particular new product and may heavily influence its design. In later representations to the ultimate consumer—through both advertising and personal contacts—marketers may also influence the ways in which the products are actually used. Therefore, marketing practices are also examined in most product-safety audits. Among the questions likely to be asked in this portion of the audit are these:

(1) Are marketing and sales personnel, at headquarters and in the field, kept fully aware of the implications of safety-related product failure?

(2) Is there a system for alerting marketing personnel to safety-related product defects and the possible consequences of such defects for users?

(3) Are marketing and advertising personnel kept aware of the product-liability exposure that could result from improper claims about product performance, reliability, applications, and so on?

(4) Are sales personnel familiar with approved product-use instructions?

(5) Are marketing and sales personnel kept aware of hazards that might arise from both normal and extraordinary product handling and use?

(6) Is there a procedure for reviewing product advertisements and collateral sales literature for their safety implications, prior to the release of this material to customers and the general public?

(7) Is there a program for training nonemployees (manufacturers' representatives, wholesalers, retailers, etc.) in the proper use of

company products and in the hazards that could result from their misuse?

(8) Has provision been made to assure that adequate product-use instructions and hazard warnings are included with the delivery of every product (e.g., as labeling on a product, as part of the packaging, or as separate materials accompanying the product)?

(9) Is there provision for regular review of the adequacy of such materials?

(10) Have all warranty statements been reviewed to ensure their conformance with the Magnuson-Moss Warranty Act—a federal statute regulating warranty descriptions and terms—and to minimize the firm's product-liability exposure?

(11) Is there a program for regularly analyzing how customers use the company's products and the potential hazards involved?

(12) Are product-design and quality-assurance personnel kept informed of reports from field sales personnel regarding product-safety problems?

(13) Are marketing personnel generally aware of the firm's obligations under various federal, state and local product-safety statutes?

(14) Are service personnel required to report safety hazards they encounter during field inspections, servicing or repair work, as well as reporting other contacts with customers that provide them with opportunities for observing the product in use?

(15) Are service and sales personnel aware that by their actions (e.g. making statements regarding product use, failing to report instances of product misuse or misapplication, etc.) they can involve the company in product-liability litigation?

(16) Are units that receive customer complaints (service or consumer affairs departments) fully acquainted with the procedures for handling those relating to product safety?

(17) Is there an adequate provision throughout the company for relaying such information quickly and efficiently to all those concerned with safety matters?

(18) Are various elements in the distribution chain (distributors, wholesalers, agents, etc.)

encouraged to maintain records systems that would facilitate any product-recall efforts that may be required?

(19) Are sales and service personnel instructed simply to report the facts on product-safety matters and not add opinions on such matters in their field reports?

General Policies and Plans

In addition to the monitoring of functional areas directly related to safety, audits should also, according to several safety executives, attempt to review the company's general policies and precautionary steps that deal with safety issues. For example, relevant questions in this area may include:

(1) Has a formal product-safety policy been developed and disseminated for the company, and are all company personnel made fully aware of its provisions?

(2) Have contingency plans been developed to deal with major product crises or environmental-safety disasters?

(3) Has a crisis team been designated to take charge in the event of such emergencies?

(4) Is there a mechanism for conducting thorough post-mortems following safety mishaps?

(5) Has corporate management made certain that safety goals and safety improvement programs are established for each of the company's operating units?

Presenting the Findings of the Safety Audit

Most often, safety executives say, a safety audit is presented to senior management in the form of a detailed report summarizing the strengths and weaknesses, as far as product safety is concerned, of the various company units examined.

Sometimes the report begins by describing an evolution of the company's safety efforts, and the safety efforts of the various units studied, thus giving management an opportunity to observe the progress—or lack of it—in various operating units. In those instances where practices fall somewhat short of full conformance to company standards, there may be extenuating circumstances that are expanded upon in the audit report. But safety executives say there is a determined effort not to lace the report with details on specific products, claims, and so on, noting that such reporting might later prove counter-productive should the audit report be obtained by persons suing the firm over an alleged safety defect.[1]

---

[1] Plaintiffs' attorneys are able, through the discovery process, to obtain, under court order, all relevant documents pertaining to a product-liability claim. The audit report could be one of those documents obtained by plaintiffs' counsel. To insulate such reports from discovery proceedings, some firms have classified the report as communications to their own counsel and direct the report to the company's chief counsel, reasoning that such communications may be privileged and immune from a discovery proceeding. But some product-liability attorneys question the validity of this practice and believe that such reports are, or should be, available to plaintiffs in product-liability litigation.

Chapter 8

Product-Safety Committees

PRODUCT-SAFETY COMMITTEES, in one form or another, are reported by a substantial minority of the companies surveyed. Usually, the work of these committees supplements or reinforces that of the full-time or part-time product-safety professionals in the companies. But in a few instances, and primarily among smaller firms and producers of nonconsumer products, the product-safety committee itself may be the sole unit in the company (or divison) charged with product-safety responsibilities (see Table 9).

Composition of Product-Safety Committees

Few product-safety committees have exactly the same mix of functions represented among the committee members. There are, however, certain departments that tend to be present on a majority of committees—legal, marketing, quality assurance, research and development, safety, and so on, (see Table 10).

In general, fewer than eight persons serve on most committees. The disciplines or departments represented depend partly on the organizational level at which a committee is situated (corporate, group, division, etc.). For example, legal and insurance specialists are most often located at the corporate level of a company, and will more likely be represented on corporate-level safety committees than on committees at the operating-unit level. And, obviously, whether or not the firm has cen-

Table 9: Companies' Reliance on Product-Safety Committees[1]

Committee Presence	In Nondivisionalized Companies	In Divisionalized Companies		
		At Corporate Level	At Group Level	At Major Division Level
Has a safety committee....................	45%	39%	19%	33%
Has no safety committee	55	61	81	67
Total...............................	100%	100%	100%	100%

[1]Based on experience of 226 companies reporting on corporate level, 179 on group level, 211 on major division level, and 49 nondivisionalized product-safety function experience.

Table 10: Composition of Product-Safety Committees

Function or Department Represented	In Nondivisionalized Companies	Percentage of Reported Committees Having Representation from Indicated Function[1] In Divisionalized Companies		
		At Corporate Level	At Group Level	At Major Division Level
Engineering..............................	77%	33%	50%	60%
Quality assurance	73	34	62	64
Production	68	27	56	73
Sales-marketing..........................	68	40	71	64
Legal	45	73	47	30
Research and development.................	36	43	44	32
Safety (product or occupational)	32	55	29	30
Finance.................................	18	11	6	4
Insurance	14	35	9	9
Administration...........................	14	22	29	23
Product design..........................	14	14	9	12
Number of Companies Reporting..........	22	88	34	69

[1]Totals may not add to 100% because of rounding.

tralized or decentralized various functions—such as quality assurance, marketing, and the like—will also affect the makeup of committees at various levels of the organization.

And in a few cases, where OSHA-type safety considerations are intermingled with product-safety concerns, employee relations, personnel, medical and similar specialists are likely to be assigned as committee members. In some instances—where there is substantial risk of damage to a company's marketplace image as a result of a product-safety failure—it is not unusual to find public relations or public affairs specialists included on the committee.

A few safety executives point out that the makeup of their committees is largely dictated by their firms' past experience with product-safety failures. For example, because the product-safety committee of one tire company is so directly involved with product recalls, it assigns warehousing and physical distribution specialists to the safety committee (along with quality assurance, law, production, product-engineering and planning specialists). This assignment reflects the committee's obvious concerns in recovering—from both company and distributor-owned storage facilities—tires believed to be safety defective.

The safety committees of retail firms frequently include both product service and merchandising specialists. This is because many safety problems involve appliance failures, and the solution to these difficulties requires the close cooperation of the merchandising and product-repair or service functions. (For example, see J.C. Penney organization chart, page 23.)

As a general rule, product-safety committees at the corporate level tend to be larger in size, including more diverse professional specialties, and tend to focus on policy issues and the coordination of product-safety efforts among various operating units. At the operating unit level, the product-safety committee more often devotes itself to a detailed examintion of the product-safety efforts of its unit, focusing on specific product-safety incidents, the evaluation of new products proposals, and so forth (see page 53).

Committee Reporting Relationships

In nearly all of the companies examined, the product-safety committee reports to the highest level of general management—most often to the president or chairman of the board. At the corporate level, product-safety committees normally report to the company president or executive vice president. At the division and group level, in a majority of instances, the committees report to the executive heading the unit. (Operating-level product-safety committees sometimes report also, on a dotted-line basis, to the corporate-level safety committee or to a corporate officer with overall responsibility for safety matters.) For examples, see pages 17 and 23.

Duties and Responsibilities

Most product-safety committees are "issue oriented." They approach safety matters using the diverse experience and viewpoints of the members to provide a multifaceted approach to solving or dealing with safety issues. The committees tend to meet on a demand basis, rather than on a fixed schedule, and often deal with exceptional safety incidents, rather than with routine safety concerns. The primary duties of safety committees commonly consist of:

(1) Helping to establish safety policies and procedures for the company (or the operating unit represented by the members).

(2) Providing consultation to top management on safety matters (in particular, developing guidelines on the safety implications inherent in product design and testing; manufacturing controls; product emergencies— including recalls, major failures, and the like; product-use instructions and labeling information; advertising; and safety-related recordkeeping.

(3) Monitoring and appraising overall safety performance.

(4) Coordinating company safety efforts with respect to product-recall campaigns; liaison with regulatory agencies; and product-liability litigation defenses; and so on.

The consultation function of the product-safety committee is one of the primary rationales for its existence. During the development of the current "product safety issue," many safety executives say, general management has recognized the need to bring together the talents and experiences of numerous kinds of specialists to deal with safety matters. One reason for the confluence of such talents in a high-level safety committee is given by a vice president of a consumer appliance firm:

"There just aren't very many individuals around with the breadth of experience and expertise needed to solve our product-safety problems. We need to call in specialists from engineering, legal, regulatory affairs, and so on, and to meld their views and efforts in order to have any realistic hope of solving the increasingly complex problems we now face in the safety field."

Similarly, the managements of other firms view a "jury opinion" as an indispensable adjunct to their own decision making on safety issues. The jury concept has appeals because it provides a mechanism to balance the often contrasting safety-related views and interests of various departments and specialists within the company.

The product-safety manager of a toy company explains that at times a few safety-committee members are tempted to be "ultraconservative" and may attempt to dissuade the company from introducing new products, even when all safety specifications have been met and all reasonable precautions taken. The committee provides a forum for the views of both "conservatives" and "liberals," reportedly producing a consensus with which senior management can feel comfortable.

Committee Role in Policy Setting

In nearly all cases, a firm's senior

management is the "official" architect of its product-safety policy. In most instances, however, the actual development of policy proposals, as well as recommendations on the procedures needed to fulfill such policies, has been the handiwork of the company's product-safety committee. Thus, safety policy is first drafted by committee and then forwarded to top management for endorsement and promulgation.

"Originally, we felt that the legal department should draft our product-safety policy," says the group vice president in a toiletries company. "But since the individual members of the safety committee are responsible for augmenting the policy, we reconsidered and gave the committee the job of writing the company's safety policy."

It is not unusual for a product-safety committee to suggest periodic revisions in safety policy. Changes in product mix, the degree of risk exposure, methods of distribution, and the like may necessitate such modifications.

In most cases, individual operating units are thought to be better able than headquarters observers to develop specific safety guidelines for their units. The most common exceptions are for procedures having companywide safety implications, at which time the corporate product-safety committee may become actively involved in drafting procedures to be followed by various operating units.

Monitoring and Evaluating Safety Performance

The vast majority of safety committees studied receive regular reports on the "safety performance" of the company (or divisions). Performance usually refers to the number and severity of safety incidents (safety-related product failures, customer claims or complaints about the safety performance of products or services, product-liability litigation, investigations or citations by state or federal safety regulators, etc.). In some instances, a corporate-level safety committee receives such information directly from the various operating divisions. In these cases, the corporate safety committee can track the statistical performance of the various groups and divisions being monitored from one time period to another. But, safety committees, at both a corporate and operating-unit level, are not only concerned with the number of safety incidents that occur, but with the implications that these incidents have for company fortunes. It is conceivable, safety executives point out, that the number of safety-related failures can be declining and yet the overall risk to the company increasing—because of the nature or severity of those incidents that are taking place.

While product-safety committees lack direct line authority over units that may be producing an "abnormal number of safety failures," they can exert considerable influence, particularly when this performance is automatically called to top management's attention through the committee's reports. And, safety executives say, it is not unusual for a committee to request that the manager of a unit having safety problems appear before the committee to explain what is going wrong.

Coordinating Company Safety Efforts

Numerous company safety efforts, whether of a routine or emergency nature, require the coordinated participation of diverse company functions—marketing, legal, quality assurance, manufacturing, and so forth. Organizationally, however, specialists in all of these areas are unlikely to report to the same executive. Thus, it is difficult to get them all to work at the same time toward similar goals.

One of the reported advantages of the product-safety committee is that it provides a "gangplank" across the organization, allowing the various departments to communicate and interact on safety issues without the normal "up and over" communication channeling that might otherwise be mandated. While advising their own superiors as to actions being taken on safety matters, they nonetheless can work in concert. Certain safety efforts in particular, such as product-recall campaigns, require extremely close coordination and timing of action by several different units in a company.

In such cases, a safety committee reportedly can help to assure a team approach, rather than a fragmented effort.

A committee sometimes is able to "look behind" overall measures of safety performance and to spot early warning signs that could spell catastrophe. "What might appear as a minor statistical aberration," one executive explains, "can have a great deal of significance to a group of experts who can visualize what this occurrence means in context of the company's many and varied risk exposures." For example, when one company began to receive several safety complaints about a newly introduced product, the company's marketing manager (a member of the safety committee) observed that the complaints seemed to fall within certain geographic areas. Quick analysis ruled out environmental factors (heat, cold, moisture, etc.) as contributing to the problem. Further investigation revealed that sales representatives in the areas had been provided incorrect instructions on the product's use and application. This erroneous advice resulted in product failure and injuries to customers.

Marketing and distribution members of the safety committee first spotted the possible difficulty. They were then able to launch an emergency reeducation program of the area's salesmen, with help from technical specialists from the engineering and consumer affairs departments also represented on the committee.

Exhibit 34: Job Description of Product-Safety Committee—Celanese Corporation

RESPONSIBLE ISSUING DEPT.:   SECTION: GENERAL ADMINISTRATION
Vice President
Personnel &
Organization   SUBJECT: Product Safety Matters

Operating Company Product Safety Committees

    (1)   Each operating group or company shall establish an Operating Company Product Safety Committee.

    (2)   Membership

        Each Operating Company Committee shall include a chairman, who shall be appointed by the company or group president, the Corporate Medical Director, the Corporate Director of Safety and Security, a representative of the Law Department, and such other members as the president of the company or group shall designate. Members should be selected to ensure that each company or group plant and office will be familiar with the activities of the Operating Company Committee and will bring to its attention matters which have product safety implications. It is recommended that the persons responsible for technical review of company literature and compliance with product safety laws and regulations be on the committee.

(3)   Functions and Procedures

(A)   Each committee shall establish procedures patterned
      after the above described procedures of the corporate
      committee. Matters which cannot await the call of a
      meeting may be reviewed by the Company Committee
      Chairman, the Corporate Medical Director, the Law
      Department representative, and any other member of the
      Operating Company Committee directly affected by the
      decision. If such persons cannot resolve the problem,
      the matter may be referred to the president of the
      operating company or his designee. If such person
      cannot resolve the matter, it may be referred to the
      corporate committee.

(B)   Each operating company committee shall establish
      procedures to evaluate and analyze the characteristics
      of new or materially altered products and of all new
      reasonably foreseeable uses of existing products to
      determine whether any such product or use will or does
      present an unreasonable risk of injury to person or
      property, including risks which might arise during
      shipping, storage and/or handling. Each operating
      company committee shall also establish procedures for
      evaluating any complaint or claim which may be made by
      a customer, consumer, or anyone else about the safety of
      any product. Such procedures should include, where
      appropriate, provisions for testing (including, but not
      necessarily limited to, toxicity, flammability, stability,
      corrosion, chemical incompatibility, etc.).

      All decisions concerning testing relating to health
      matters shall be approved through the Corporate Medical
      Director, and all decisions concerning testing relating
      to safety matters shall be approved through the Corporate
      Safety and Security Director.

(C)   Each committee shall also establish procedures for the
      dissemination of information, where appropriate, outlining
      potential dangers from the shipping, storage, handling or
      use of its products, including samples and intermediates.
      Such information may include, but is not necessarily limited
      to, product labels, material safety data sheets, technical
      bulletins, educational pamphlets and advertising.

No product, including samples and intermediates, shall be shipped outside a plant or laboratory, or offered for sale, advertised or described in operating company or corporation literature without inclusion of all safety and health information required by the operating company committee.

(D) Operating company committee procedures shall also include provision for continual review of applicable laws and regulations to ensure that each operating company is meeting its legal responsibilities. Each operating company committee is responsible for the approval of each new or materially altered product and each new end use for its products. Each request for approval shall be in writing.

(E) Each operating company committee shall develop a form for such requests. The form shall be designed to elicit all information necessary to enable the committee to evaluate the product effectively. The form should require, but should not necessarily be limited to, all applicable available health, safety, and regulatory compliance information on the product and its proposed uses. Where appropriate, it should also require attachment of any proposed label and other pertinent literature which will be distributed with the product. New information concerning the potential danger of a product, its shipping, storage, handling or use, or any new or additional literature about a product must be reviewed by the committee.

(F) All procedures adopted by operating companies or groups shall be approved by the corporate committee before becoming effective. Each operating company or group committee's minutes shall be distributed to all members of the corporate committee for information.

Committees in Smaller Companies: The Tennant Company

Product-safety committees have proved valuable to many moderate-sized firms. The smaller firm often relies on the safety committee for monitoring safety conditions and coordinating safety efforts because its scale of operations does not permit the establishment of elaborate product-safety arrangements.

The experience of The Tennant Company is typical of a number of such surveyed. At Tennant, the product-safety committee is comprised of individuals from the engineering, product design, chemistry, marketing research, plant safety, quality-assurance, and finance departments. The committee meets regularly every six weeks, but gets together more often if required. Subcommittees screen the agenda topics for the full committee. According to a company spokesman, the principal goals of the committee are: "First, to make certain that accidents don't happen; and, second, to determine that the company has done everything possible to avoid those injuries which do occur."

Tennant safety-committee members are required to provide alternate delegates if they are unable to attend one of the committee meetings. The committee has no veto power over such activities as new-product introductions, product-line modifications, and so on. But it reportedly enjoys such high credibility and respect that an operating manager is extremely unlikely to ignore its recommendations.

A Housewares Producer's Use of Product-Safety Committees

The management of one housewares manufacturer believes it essential for the company's product-safety committee to be insulated from an intimate concern with—or even knowledge of—day-to-day operations, budget, profit and loss considerations, and the like in arriving at product-safety decisions. The assertion is that the committee members should be making their decisions on as an objective basis as possible with minimum concern over the potential dollar impact that their decisions may have.

For this review, the company deliberately selects a heterogeneous group of "non-experts" to serve on the product-safety committee. There are five outsiders—a local physician's wife, the wife of an insurance agent, the head of a homemakers service, a local retailer, and the head of a local ambulance service. Members from inside the company currently include the corporate insurance manager, a consumer correspondent, a chemist and the chief steward of the executive dining room.

The key selection criteria for these committee members, a spokesman says, has been their ability to ask hard questions and to be skeptical of easy solutions to product-failure issues.

The product-safety committee meets approximately ten times a year and an agenda prepared in advance by the firm's manager of consumer affairs is provided committee members a week prior to each meeting. At the meeting, new items for inclusion on the next meeting's agenda are submitted by committee members.

The committee receives a quarterly report from the consumer affairs department detailing the number and types of product-failure incidents known to that department. This tally also records the number of incidents in which injuries occurred during use of specific products. After examining the report, committee members probe those situations that seem most significant. A qualified technical person from the division producing a product thought to pose safety problems provides a technical explanation of the product failures.

The company's hopes of avoiding product failure are reflected in the screening process for new products. A quality assurance representative reviews all product prototypes while they are still in the design stage. A separate product evaluation department, staffed with home economists, checks to see how consumers are likely to use—or perhaps misuse—proposed products and then determines what kinds of injuries might conceivably result from such misuse or abuse.

Safety considerations for new products are also examined by the use of a service test panel. The members are 2,700 families living in adjacent communities, none of whom are employees or related to employees of the company. Field service representatives monitor and consult with the panelists about the products' performance, paying particular attention to safety-related shortcomings. The product-safety committee has access to all of the service test findings.

The division's senior consumer affairs executive sees its product-safety committee as "a kind of board of directors that oversees the way we are managing our product-safety effort." He goes on to state, "All of us try to be as objective as possible, but we can't walk on water—we can't completely divorce ourselves from our company ties. The product-safety committee, because of its outside representation and heterogeneous makeup, imparts the degree of objectivity to our decision making that might not otherwise be possible."

Charter for a Product-Safety Committee

The formal charter described below is a composite example based on several such charters as established by the companies surveyed. (Only a minority of reporting firms—primarily consumer goods producers have charters for their product-safety committees.)

"The product-safety committee will be comprised of the principal executives from the manufacturing, quality assurance, insurance, legal, research and development, and product-safety departments. The permanent chairman of the committee will be the product-safety manager. The product-safety committee will meet on a regular schedule as established by committee members, and will report the results of its meetings to the executive vice president in the form of detailed minutes to be kept for each meeting.

"The committee will provide advice and counsel to the company's senior management on topical product-safety matters and will report on the overall product performance of the firm's products and divisions with regard to safety matters. The product-safety committee will have the following specific duties and responsibilities:

"(1) In consultation with marketing and technical personnel, the committee will establish guidelines and criteria by which the safety potential of the company's products may be assessed. In establishing such standards, and monitoring adherence to these standards, the committee will seek to determine the normal usage of the company's products and the hazards associated with both their normal application and potential misuse.

"(2) The committee will develop standards and procedures for responding to product complaints involving actual or potential injury to users of the company's products. It will also establish an information gathering and analysis system to guarantee that information relating to product-safety hazards comes to the immediate attention of appropriate operating personnel.

"(3) The committee will review all printed literature—such as that used for advertising, promotion or product-use instruction purposes—that might influence the way in which customers use the company's products; and it will assess the accuracy, appropriateness and potential impact of this information with respect to the safetyworthiness of the products.

"(4) The committee will review local, state and federal product-safety regulations and report on their relevance and applicability to the company's existing or proposed products."

Exhibit 35: Consumer Affairs Department, Consumer Products Division—A Housewares Manufacturer

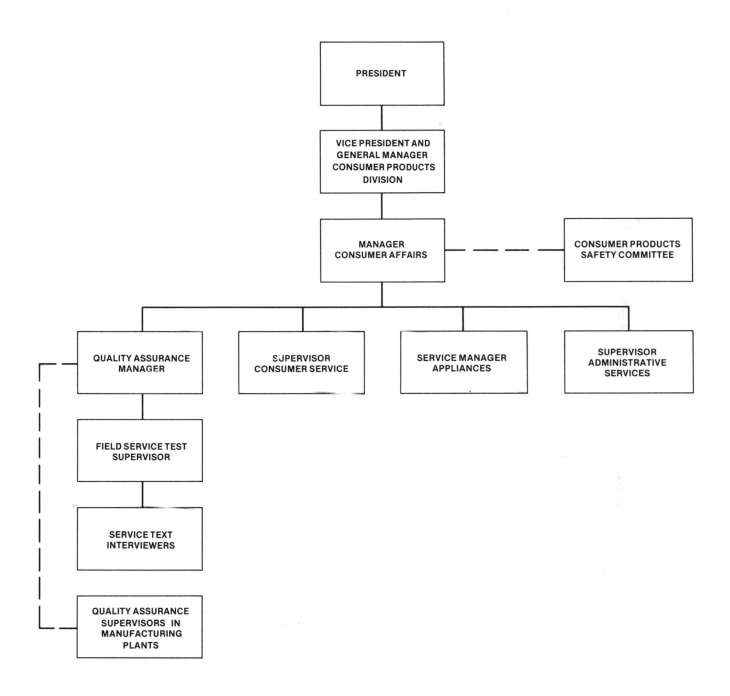

Chapter 9

Product-Safety Policies

FORMAL policy statements, delineating company action and philosophy with regard to product safety, have been established by a majority of the responding companies. The actual scope and detail of these policy statements, as well as their philosophical content and tone, differs a great deal from one company to another. Similarly, some statements focus only on policy issues, while others incorporate matters which are primarily practice and procedure topics (descriptions of job responsibility and reporting relationships, response to safety incidents, and so forth).

The Pros and Cons of Formal Policy Statements

A minority of company managements believe that it is not necessary—or, in fact, may even be undesirable—for their companies to have broad, fixed guidelines on product safety. Reporting executives in such firms cite the following as rationale for avoiding the formulation of clear-cut product-safety policy statements.

(1) A company's obligation to produce safe products, in the opinion of these managements, is implicit and needs no formal description—as in the case of its obligations to adhere to all laws with respect to safety, or any other matters.

Thus, the inclusion of such statements of policy on these subjects in their corporate policy manuals is seen as superfluous.

(2) Formal, and particularly detailed, statements of a company's policy and procedures with regard to product safety may hamstring firms because these statements may excessively narrow the latitude of decision making. There are numerous "gray areas" in product safety where, it is claimed, executives need maximum judgmental freedom. The detailed statement—especially when procedures are minutely described—may slow or complicate a company's response to a critical safety issue.

(3) Some executives say that broadly written policy statements rarely have much impact on the conduct of company employees, who have grown "immune" to what are regarded as platitudes about corporate good citizenship. Such statements, these executives say, are habitually ignored by operating managers.

On the other hand, a majority of managements believe it desirable to spell out the company's position on product safety through formal statements of policy, often on the grounds that ensuring safe products "has to start somewhere, and the drafting of a formal policy statement is the most logical first step." Primary reasons given in support of this action include the following:

(1) There are certain areas in which the company has broad societal obligations—such as providing equal employment opportunities, protecting the environment, and product safety—where it is both necessary and advantageous to reinforce the firm's position in a formal way, and and make certain that those concerned parties inside and outside the company hear its "official voice" on the subject.

(2) It is desirable to put company employees, at all levels, on formal notice that the company intends to produce and market safe products, and that violations of this intent will not be tolerated by management. Among other things, policy statements serve to remind managers that their overall performance will be assessed in part by how well they insure conformance to the company's product-safety policy.

(3) Formal product-safety policies, in the opinion of some executives, can perhaps be used to legal advantage on occasion, if it can be clearly shown, in the event of a product failure, that an employee has flagrantly ignored company directives regarding product-safety policies and procedures and must, therefore, shoulder some personal blame for the failure. (As a point of law, of course, a business may still be held responsible for the torts of its employees, but the existence of a formal policy, it is argued, can sometimes be used as "evidence of good faith" in a presentation to the court; and thus may have a mitigating influence on the punitive damages that might be awarded in a product-liability suit.) The existence of policy guidelines is also said to be helpful in convincing government regulators that a firm is serious about its responsibilities to maintain the safety of its products.

(4) If properly formulated, policy statements regarding product safety may help to eliminate potentially dangerous confusion between staff and operating units about their respective responsibilities for meeting product-safety standards.

Who Drafts Product-Safety Policy?

Formulating a policy statement is a task often assigned to a company's chief product-safety executive. But, as noted previously, product-safety committees also have a major role in such policy formation. A draft prepared by product-safety specialists, or safety committees, is generally reviewed by the company's chief legal officer, as well as the executive to whom the safety executive or committee reports, and ultimately is approved by the company's chief executive.

In a few reported instances, a company's product-safety policy was written by its legal department, sometimes aided by communications specialists from the public relations department. But regardless of the origin of the document, or the functional titles of its authors, the draft must receive the imprimatur of the corporation's top management.

Policy statements are seldom regarded as static instruments. As company circumstances alter—sometimes as a result of product-liability litigation or new safety regulations—there may be a need to amend, delete or enlarge portions of the policy.

Among the companies studied, there is evidence of a trend toward expanding policy statements on safety, so as to define more precisely the roles of various company officers vis-à-vis product safety. At one chemicals firm, such amendments were spurred by a newly active board of directors that had become restive over various aspects of officers' and directors' liability. The members asked the company's product-safety committee to spell out in greater detail the responsibility of various officers of the company on safety-connected issues. (They also wanted more details to be given them on specific safety problems such as product recalls, liability litigation, and any fines that might be imposed by regulatory agencies.)

Elements of Product-Safety Policy

The typical safety-policy guideline begins with a generalized statement regarding the company's commitment to produce and market products that provide optimum safety for their users. Then, the guideline usually goes on to affirm the company's desire to comply with all laws and regulations—state, federal and local—relating to product safety.

There is often also an affirmation of the company's intent to take all reasonable steps, as might be instituted by prudent management, to protect its reputation and assets through the production and marketing of safe products. As a corollary, it states the responsibility of all individuals employed by the company to help guarantee the safety of its products and to adhere to all applicable safety laws.

Subsequent portions of the safety policy tend to become more detailed, defining ways in which generalized safety goals will be met. For example, it is here that the specific responsibilities of the product-safety function, or possibly the product-safety committee, may be cited and its reporting and working relationship within the company defined. In multidivision firms, corporate policy may specify divisional authority in safety matters.

The provisions of some firms' safety policies cover the required evaluation of product proposals, the determination of risk potential, the follow-up on safety failures that may occur, and the education of employees regarding safety standards and procedures.

Disclaimers and Limitations

The prudent influence of legal counsel can sometimes be observed in the drafting of a firm's policy statement. The evidence is found in the presence of disclaimers and limitations included in an attempt to confine the company's safety responsibilities to those actions that can be "reasonably" expected of the business' management. In addition, it is not uncommon to find policies setting down the limitations of safety responsibility to situations involving "normally intended usages, or reasonably foreseeable misuse" of products "maintained in reasonable operating conditions," and so on. Such provisos are visible attempts to shield a company from possible litigation by customers who deliberately, or unknowingly, misuse the product, are injured as a result, and then seek damages.

While it is an established tenet that ignorance of the law is no defense for its violation, a few policy statements appear to be attempts to limit a company's safety responsibilities to those statutes or regulations that have been "published or which the company has been apprised of." Some observers see such wording as an effort to protect the company against troubles that might ensue from good-faith ignorance of ambiguous safety regulations, or ones that may have only recently been reinterpreted by a regulatory agency.

Professional opinion varies as to whether these or other disclaimers are helpful or useless in protecting a company against various forms of safety-involved litigation. But there is a recognition, too, that product-safety policies are sometimes more palatable to company managers when they contain such provisions.

Examples of Policy Statements

On pages 95—101 are several examples of product safety policies, some for very large corporations, others for relatively small firms. Each is a unique document, designed to fill the special needs and philosophy of the company that issues the statement.

<u>COMPANY PRODUCT SAFETY POLICY</u>

<u>Background</u>

Providing products that are reliable and safe for their intended use and reasonably foreseeable misuse and that meet the needs of our customers is a corporate responsibility of PPG Industries, Inc. Acceptance of this responsibility throughout the company is essential to preserve confidence of customers, retain their business, and compete successfully in the marketplace. Moreover, meeting this responsibility supports our corporate objective of "Concern For The Future" by providing products and services that improve the quality of life.

It is appropriate to unify formally in a statement of corporate policy the various areas of concern for product safety. The need for sharper focus and corporate communication arises from a number of factors, among which are the introduction of new and more complex products, the rapid expansion into new areas of endeavor, the high rate of technological change and the rising concern and expectations of the public regarding product safety.

The intent of this policy is to emphasize the importance of continuing attention to customer needs and expectations concerning product safety (product reliability, quality and environmental effects) and to define objectives and responsibilities for the design, manufacture, test, transportation, installation, maintenance and disposal of products that meet or exceed appropriate standards.

<u>Policy & Objectives</u>

It is the policy of PPG INDUSTRIES, INC. to provide products and services which:

(1) Perform their required function safely for their intended use and reasonably foreseeable misuse.

(2) Perform their required function reliably and with minimum adverse effects on the environment.

(3) Meet or exceed applicable federal, state and local regulations and industry standards.

(4) Meet consumer needs and reasonable expectations where safety laws or regulations or industry standards do not exist.

(5) Offer minimum risk of injury to persons, property and the environment.

(6) Are accurately advertised, labeled and promoted and are properly packaged, and handled by PPG, shippers and customers.

```
CORPORATE POLICY

PRODUCT SAFETY
```

PURPOSE: To establish a corporatewide posture on product safety.

SCOPE: The company, including all its operating divisions and
                    majority-owned subsidiary corporations.

POLICY   The corporation will implement programs designed to
STATEMENT: avoid injury, sickness, or death to persons, and damage
                    to property and the environment which may result from
                    development, design, manufacture, marketing, installation,
                    service, use, or disposal of its products and/or services.
                    These programs will give due regard to applicable federal,
                    state, local, and industry safety standards, regulatory
                    requirements, technology state-of-the-art and conventional
                    standards and constraints as may bear on the corporation's
                    activities.

ADMINISTRATION:

Product   –   Maintain surveillance over all company operations
Safety   to assure conformance to the above policy.
Review   –   Recommend programs or actions, both preventive and
Committee   corrective, to senior and division managements in
                    cases of significant product safety exposure or
                    experience.

Division   –   Establish controls over product quality, safety,
Management   marketing, advertising, warranting, usage, and recall.
                –   Assure policy compliance in the introduction of new
                    or modified products and/or uses.
                –   Obtain and use product safety expertise from
                    appropriate staff departments.
                –   Delegate to appropriate levels of subordinate
                    management and personnel managerial and operational
                    responsibility for conformance with product safety
                    policy and procedures, and monitor and control
                    compliance.

Subordinate   –   Comply with established product safety policy and
Managerial and   procedures.
Operational
Personnel

1/ Company name withheld at firm's request.

Exhibit 38: Excerpt from Corporate Policy on Product Safety—Brunswick Corporation

CORPORATE POLICY: Health and Safety--Product Safety

SCOPE: This policy applies to all Brunswick locations, divisions and subsidiaries of the corporation.

SUPERSEDES: All previous regulations on this subject.

I NEED FOR A POLICY

(A) Providing safe, reliable products and services is of great importance to Brunswick Corporation.

(B) Consistent with this need, providing safe products and services is essential in order to fulfill our corporate responsibilities to the public, to remain competitive and to retain customers' confidence and business.

(C) All manufacturers of products have a responsibility to produce products that satisfy the safety expectations of society. These expectations have recently accelerated with the result that safety must receive more emphasis than ever before in decisions concerning the design, production, and marketing of products including ultimate intended use and reasonably foreseeable misuse.

(D) The intent of this policy is to emphasize the importance of continuing attention to customer needs and expectations concerning product integrity.

II STATEMENT OF POLICY

(A) It is a policy of Brunswick Corporation:

(1) To take the practical steps necessary and do all that is reasonable to prevent injury or damage and loss to persons or property from the products and services it provides giving full regard to applicable industry standards, regulatory requirements, technological developments and the standards of care required by society.

(2) To emphasize the importance of product safety; to establish guidelines for identifying product accident potential and preventing or minimizing possible harmful effects by establishing responsibilities and accountability for product safety actions and results.

Exhibit 38: Excerpt from Corporate Policy on Product Safety—Brunswick Corporation (continued)

(3) To have the top ranking executive at each division directly responsible for the manufacture and sale of safe products consistent with corporate policies and guidelines; for implementing and establishing a products safety program and to delegate to the appropriate staff member the day-to-day responsibility for the administration of the products safety program.

(4) To have the top-ranking executive of the organization at each division appoint a Products Safety Committee and authorize it to implement a division products safety program consistent with corporate policy and guidelines appropriate to the products or services produced or offered for sale by the division.

(5) To have the top-ranking executive of the organization at each division specifically responsible for taking prompt action to comply with all applicable product safety laws, standards, codes and ordinances; for issuance and enforcement of division procedures implementing this policy and for establishing and conducting product safety programs which are in general conformance to the corporate guidelines.

Exhibit 39: Excerpts from Policy Statement on Business Conduct and Safety—Aluminum Company of America

Alcoa Policy Guidelines for Business Conduct

Alcoans have always set a high standard of behavior for themselves. We have been guided by internal policies, both written and unwritten. Today, Alcoa and its affiliate companies operate plants and sell goods in many countries. We intend that Alcoa will conduct its affairs everywhere in the world according to the highest standards of personal and corporate performance. We start with the law, wherever we operate. Our policy is to obey it. Alcoa intends that its business and the actions of all Alcoans will represent the real spirit and intent of the laws and moral codes under which we operate and live. Form and appearance *are* important. We want and expect Alcoans to do what is right. And even beyond that, we expect Alcoans to act so that others will view them as having the very highest standards of personal and corporate behavior.

Our principle is integrity, and we pledge ourselves to be honest in our relationships with each other, with individuals outside the company and with other organizations, both public and private. Simply stated, this means no employee will be allowed to abuse Alcoa's good name with any illegal or unethical act to obtain special favors or consideration from any person or any organization. There can be no exceptions. Alcoans must not have improper dealings with suppliers, customers or competitors. We will not buy off or pay off anyone to further corporate goals. Nor will we accept gifts or favors that might influence, or be expected to influence, our dealings with others. This applies to the company, to all of its divisions and subsidiaries, and to every employee throughout the world.

Every officer, every manager and every supervisor has a special responsibility to act in accord with our policies, to communicate these, to set a standard of performance for all employees they supervise, and, as necessary, to enforce these policies.

Ultimately, there is no way to assure behavior except through the desire of the individual. And there is no way to prescribe rules of conduct that will apply to every possible situation. All we can do is to establish a broad code of conduct that sets minimum goals and describes in detail guidelines to cover the most common and the most sensitive activities. That we have done.

We have recently completed a reexamination of these guidelines and of Alcoa's fundamental objectives, principles and policies. What follows are statements of those. Every Alcoan is expected to accept personal responsibility for following and implementing these policy guidelines. We believe they reflect the kind of company Alcoa is. They certainly reflect the way we expect every Alcoan to perform on the job.

Alcoa's Fundamental Objectives

Aluminum Company of America, as a broadly owned multinational company, is committed to four fundamental, interdependent objectives, all of which are essential to its long-term success. The ideas behind these words have been part of Alcoa's success for many years—as has the company's intention to excel in all these objectives:

• Provide for shareholders a return superior to that available from other investments of equal risk, based on reliable long-term growth in earnings per share;
• Provide employees a rewarding and challenging employment environment with

opportunity for economic and personal growth;
• Provide worldwide customers with products and services of quality;
• Direct its skills and resources to help solve the major problems of the societies and communities of which it is a part, while providing these societies with the benefits of its other fundamental objectives.

Supporting Principles—In achieving its fundamental objectives, Alcoa endorses these supporting principles and pledges to:

• Conduct its business in a legal and ethical manner;
• Provide leadership and support for the free market system through successfully achieving its corporate objectives, superiority in product development and production, integrity in its commercial dealings, active awareness of its role in society, and appropriate communication with all employees and with the public.
• Maintain a working environment that will assure each employee the opportunity for growth, for achievement of his or her personal goals, and for contributing to the achievement of the corporate goals;
• Without regard to race, color, national origin, handicap or sex, recruit, employ and develop individuals of competence and skills commensurate with job requirements;
• Make a positive contribution to the quality of life of the communities and societies in which it operates, always mindful of its economic obligations, as well as the environmental and economic impact of its activities in these communities;
• For the well-being of all employees at all locations, maintain safe and healthful working conditions, conducive to job satisfaction and high productivity.

Industrial Hygiene Protection

Maintenance of a healthy workplace in order to protect each employee from potentially harmful agents in the working environment is a basic premise underlying all Alcoa operations. This is achieved by:

• Periodic evaluations of the workplace for early detection of environmental conditions that might prove detrimental to employee health;

• Institution of appropriate controls to minimize employee work exposures to potentially harmful conditions, in accordance with good industrial hygiene practice;

• Training Alcoans to recognize the potential health hazards in their jobs and the means of avoiding undue exposure;

• Assessing and recommending personal protection devices and providing instructions for their use and care;

• Active industrial hygiene support of joint labor-management safety and health committees;

• Cooperation with local, state and federal government agencies charged with employee health protection so as to aid in the development of sound and effective standards and the development of common goals.

Product Safety and Reliability

It is Alcoa's policy to deliver to its customers safe and reliable products. To that end, the company strives:

• To design, test and manufacture products in accordance with applicable quality and safety standards and in conformance with specifications;

• To refrain from advertising, recommending or selling for a known use any product that embodies known characteristics that will render the product unsuitable or unsafe for that use;

• To provide information concerning the characteristics of products to enable customers to determine their suitability and safety for intended use;

• To make no claim for any product that is not true.

Environmental Protection

It is Alcoa's policy:

• To take necessary steps to prevent or abate harmful pollution resulting from Alcoa operations;

• To train and make available at operating locations qualified personnel whose responsibility is to bring and keep pollution under control;

• To develop improved methods to control the quality of air and water and to make that technology available to other interested companies;

• To work and cooperate with local, state and national governmental agencies charged with pollution control;

• To assist governmental bodies in the development of sound, equitable and realistic standards designed to control the quality of air and water.

GENERAL CORPORATE POLICY

PRODUCT LIABILITY

I.   SCOPE

This policy is applicable to all divisions of the parent company
and to all subsidiaries in North America engaged in the manufacture
of a product or products which can be sold and/or leased. In addition, this policy is applicable to any unit of the company that
might act as a distributor for a product which is not manufactured
by Ex-Cell-O Corporation.

II. INTRODUCTION

Recent and dramatic developments in the court decisions which influence, and the laws which govern, product liability; together with
the rapid growth of consumer awareness; have imposed far greater
responsibilities on Ex-Cell-O Corporation in the areas of design,
manufacture and the marketing of our products.

While Ex-Cell-O Corporation has always endeavored to manufacture
safe, reliable products, these trends have necessitated the establishment of a loss control program which will eliminate, so far as
possible, the risk of product liability claims and losses. As a
function of management, comprehensive product liability protection
programs must be implemented at all corporate locations.

III. PURPOSE

The purpose of this policy is to provide all personnel involved in
the design, development, manufacture, marketing, sales and advertising of products manufactured, sold and serviced by Ex-Cell-O
Corporation with the guidelines that are necessary to minimize the
corporation's exposure to product liability losses.

IV. POLICY

It is and shall continue to be the policy of Ex-Cell-O Corporation
to provide our customers with safe and reliable products. Our
employees must be committed to fulfilling the needs of our customers
and to minimizing losses in doing so. It is corporate policy that
each unit of the company is responsible for implementing a product
liability program which will ensure the continued surveillance over
product design, development, manufacture, promotion and sale, and
for coordinating these efforts to prevent the occurrence of product
liability losses.

Chapter 10

Recommendations for Establishing a Product-Safety Function

DRAWING on their personal and professional experiences, and those of their companies, senior safety executives in the companies surveyed proffered several recommendations to managements in other firms who might be contemplating the establishment of a formal product-safety function, or the reorganization of an existing unit. In general, there was substantial agreement on the primary suggestions—but, as might be anticipated, some of the recommendations occasionally proved contradictory. The box below lists the primary recommendations of safety professionals in establishing a product-safety function, in a rank-order fashion.

Naturally, relatively few firms will be starting a safety unit "completely from scratch." In most, safety responsibilities have been, and are at present, being met by an existing unit or executive. Thus, the safety executives' recommendations are idealized to a certain extent. Nonetheless, the "ideals" they present might prove useful to managements concerned with product-safety organization and operations.

Obtain Top Management's Support

It is of primary importance, product-safety executives believe, that there be continuing, clear-cut and enthusiastic support of product-safety efforts from top management. Gaining

---

Recommendations for Establishing a Product-Safety Function (in rank order of frequency of mention)

Recommendation

• Obtain full support of firm's top management

• Centralize authority and responsibility for product safety

• Involve all company units in safety effort

• Develop an extensive safety data base, particularly with regard to product standards and regulations

• Construct a companywide safety policy

• Develop a product-safety committee

• Make operating units responsible for safety performance

• Develop a capacity to measure and monitor safety performance.

---

such backing is viewed as one of the first priorities in establishing a product-safety function. In the view of safety executives, senior corporate officers must be thoroughly convinced of the importance of the product-safety function and be willing to provide wholehearted commitment to its establishment and operation. Otherwise, the activity could well come to be viewed as just another source of overhead expense.

The executives also point out that it is not enough for senior management to affirm its support of the safety function; rather, that endorsement must be widely communicated so that everyone in the company realizes the priority being given to the task of insuring safe products. Some say the personal commitment of the company's chief executive officer is needed. In a metals company, it reportedly was not until the CEO had personally lectured lagging or recalcitrant divisional vice presidents that a new safety program got on stream.

Safety executives point out that middle management, in particular, is acutely sensitive as to whether or not a new policy or program is merely a "showpiece" effort or has genuine substance and top-management backing. Moreover, the safety executives say, all the lectures, memos and other entreaties delivered by members of the company's legal or quality-assurance departments on the desirability of improved product-safety performance are not nearly so effective as a direct order from the highest ranking executive.

Concentrated Authority

A substantial number of safety specialists believe that if a company were starting from scratch in establishing a formal product-safety function, one of the best approaches would be to begin by creating a corporate-level product-safety unit and giving it a sufficient autonomy and authority to fulfill its initial mission. These executives are concerned over two organizational bugaboos: (1) that the safety effort may be so fragmented in some firms as to wield relatively little influence and; (2) that if it

is not positioned high enough in the organizational structure, and does not gain sufficient visibility, it will not have the authority necessary to accomplish its objectives.

Another common view is that expressed by a paper company executive, who says: "Product-safety duties should not be left to a committee, or be tacked on as an added responsibility to some other function." There is some fear, too, that unless a sufficient independence is provided for it, a newly established unit may find some of its goals being pushed aside by sales or production considerations. One safety manager notes: "It is vital that the function be organized so that no other function can override product-safety considerations for narrow business reasons."

Involvement of Other Company Units

Expressing a somewhat opposing view, a minority of the executives surveyed would suggest, as a first step, the appointing of product-safety specialists for each operating unit, leaving ultimate responsibility for product safety as close as possible to the point of control—that is, production, design, and so on. However, some of these same executives are not opposed to a corporate-level unit providing a coordination function for the various operating-unit safety specialists.

At least one executive suggests that it could be an advantage to "start at the lowest level and work up." Others maintain that, in many firms, safety concerns are so diverse, and so scattered, that a newly established safety unit—at a centralized location—could not possibly be expected to be able to monitor so diverse a mixture of products and operations. Thus, these executives would opt for beginning the safety effort at an operating-unit level.

Information Bases

One appropriate goal for a newly established product-safety unit is the monitoring of federal, state and local safety regulations directly affecting the company's operations. Next, safety executives suggest, all relevant trade associations and other standards-setting groups should be contacted to find out what specifications relating to product safety currently exist and should be taken into consideration. At the outset, there should be consultation between safety specialists and the firm's legal function to establish the scope of liabilities the company could face as a result of product miscues.

The safety executives surveyed believe that this data-gathering phase is vital in the establishment of a new safety unit. "You have to be able to define the task, to get some benchmarks, before you can begin building a staff, assigning priorities, and so on," one safety manager declares.

Constructing A Safety Policy

Regardless of whether or not a company decides it needs a formal product-safety function, safety executives are mostly in agreement that its safety responsibilities should be defined in a written policy. (See pages 92—94 regarding the pros and cons of such policies.) In addition, they argue for the drafting of a procedure statement that would describe the steps to be followed in major product-safety crises—such as recalls, litigation, regulatory prosecution, and the like. The executives believe such procedure outlines should get primary attention from a newly set up safety department. They maintain that the formulation of such procedures is an educational experience in itself, and it often proves valuable in pinpointing the organizational needs of the new safety unit.

The Committee Approach

As reported, a number of companies rely almost entirely on product-safety committees to oversee safety programs and meet product-safety responsibilities. A number of the executives surveyed saw the committee approach as an ideal beginning step for launching a formal product-safety effort. Of course, many would proceed further. The advice of a food company executive is:

"Begin by issuing a safety policy; then appoint a safety-review committee to examine both new and existing products. Continue the review with quality-assurance and manufacturing procedures, paying special attention to test procedures."

In several cases, executives favoring the appointment of a committee as an initial step also believe that, at minimum, senior executives from marketing, legal, manufacturing, research and development, and product-service departments should be included as members of the committee. Some went further, deeming it important to have at least one representative of general management to act as chairman.

Another executive suggested that the newly appointed committee be organized in two tiers. The first would be an evaluation group to handle most product-safety matters. But major issues—for example, those potentially involving a substantial impact on the company—would be passed on to the senior or second tier of the committee—which would be convened only on a demand basis.

Achieving Safety Involvement and Accountability

In the view of some safety specialists, the most effective product-safety program is one that involves managers and workers at all levels of the company. As one of them states: "You must start by having all employees accept the fact that product safety is an integral part of their jobs and in this way get safety designed into the product." Further, another says: "A company must hold product-line management to strict accountability for safety."

This approach to safety accountability puts primary stress on the role of the formal product-safety unit, operating as a coordinating and advising group. In the event of a safety breakdown, it is the operating managers—not a staff of safety specialists—who bear primary responsibility for responding to and correcting the safety mishap.

Establishing a Monitoring Function

For many new safety units, an early step is the establishment of controls to assist top management in spotting potential safety problems before they become major issues and disasters. The goal, as a packaging company executive notes, is "an aggressive monitoring program, one that makes certain that all systems have regulatory checkpoints."

The aim of such programs is to develop a capacity that allows management to detect safety mistakes early on. This is the type of error that often may be hidden from senior management's view.

Checking the Safetyworthiness of New Products

Since the risks associated with new products—in particular, the risk of safety failure—seem to be more numerous than for established products, there is a decided preference among safety specialists for scrutinizing this area with particular care. Safety executives recommend, in establishing or revamping a safety unit, that particular cognizance be taken of the unit's relationship to the new-product development and introduction process.

Getting Started Now

Organizing for product safety is viewed by safety executives as a matter of real urgency. Too many firms, it is maintained, "study the problem to death." Meanwhile, the risk to both customer and consumer mounts. The advice of safety executives to managements that may be considering establishing a formal function is simply: "Begin at once—don't delay."

Automated Product-Safety Data Bases

For many years trial attorneys have recognized that the ability to retrieve pertinent documents rapidly is an invaluable asset in litigation requiring the use of thousands of documents. Retrieval systems now exist that enable a lawyer to automatically obtain document directories, and indexes of key words or phrases, on subjects pertinent to litigation they are preparing.

A few companies have begun to employ similar approaches to product-safety issues and are building data bases useful in defending product-liability suits. Principally, these are chemicals and pharmaceuticals manufacturers.

One attorney and information specialist familiar with such systems cites the following as their principal advantages:

(1) They provide a readily acceptable data resource on a company's varied product experience, especially with regard to how the numerous products comply with state and federal safety regulations.

(2) The data base guarantees that information vital to the defense of a product-liability suit does not "evaporate" in the files of various departments or divisions, or remain solely in the minds of employees, who might retire or resign.

(3) The data system assists management in developing an early-warning system, a system that allows it to match mounting product-liability problems with a particular product, line or service.

(4) Once such a system is in place, it greatly reduces the costs of storing safety data, and then retrieving such information.[1]

Among the primary data that might be included in the computer file are:

(1) A listing of all state and federal regulations that apply to company products or services and the ways in which these regulations apply.

(2) Basic design and manufacturing data on all company products subject to safety regulation.

(3) Quality assurance manuals and procedures, along with basic quality-assurance data on products suspected of being safety defective.

(4) Relevant internal memoranda concerning product-safety issues.

(5) External correspondence with regulatory agencies, individual customers, suppliers, and so forth, regarding product-safety matters.

(6) The full text of all product-safety investigatory reports.

(7) Data regarding individual product-safety incidents, claims made and paid, suits defended, and so on.

(8) Data on all products recalled, including basic information on how, and to whom, the product was distributed, a roster of advertising claims made, test market reports, and so forth.

Safety specialists recommend that such projects begin as joint efforts with company information specialists who will develop a suitable coding system that will allow a variety of abstract and document data to be encoded with a minimum amount of keypunching. Computer specialists can assign key word indexes, and develop cross-tabulation programs, permitting attorneys, product-safety researchers, and so on to recover all information pertinent to a particular product-safety investigation rapidly.

[1]L. H. Berul, "Building a Data-Base Defense Against Product Liability." *Management Review*, November, 1977, pp. 18-20.

Chapter 11

Safety Efforts— Impediments and Trends

NUMEROUS FACTORS inside and outside a company may act to impede the effectiveness of its attempts to improve the safety of its products. The safety experts surveyed believe that those factors outside the company include the actions and attitudes of governmental safety regulators; time diverted to legal suits and regulatory hearings; customers' misuse of products; the lack of industrywide standards for product design and reliability; (see box below.)

Principal Impediments Safety Professionals See to Improving Product-Safety Efforts (ranked by frequency of mention)

Impediment

- Regulations and regulators

- Product testing and evaluation

- Altering company attitudes

- Product liability problems

- Increasing product complexity

- Costs and staffing problems

- Lack of proper organization

- Miscellaneous technical problems.

Inside the company, the executives see as major problems the difficulties faced in testing and evaluating how safe products actually are; in maintaining quality-assurance standards; in holding down the costs of raising or maintaining the safety of products; in assigning responsibilities for product safety, and so forth. There is worry, as well, over difficulties encountered in educating management and other company personnel about safety issues.

Problems With Regulations and Regulators

Many safety executives believe that they are "inundated" by the number of federal and state safety statutes they must pay attention to. Simply keeping up with existing and new safety requirements is a major task. (Occasional conflicts between contradictory state and federal statutes are said to add to the problems of some.)

In addition to keeping abreast of safety statutes and regulations, the safety professionals are usually expected to contribute to forecasting the kinds of new laws that may be in the offing. This responsibility often creates some strains, since new safety legislation is continuously being hatched simultaneously in numerous federal and state legislative bodies. For one firm, the main safety worry results from "the adoption of federal and state products standards, without the regulatory agencies first having adequate knowledge of the likely effect of each standard and without adequate concern for the accompanying societal cost of each standard."

At the same time, there is a generous amount of criticism directed at a number of safety regulations already on the books. One quality assurance director says: "Many federal rules and regulations are poorly thought out and result in low cost-benefit gains for consumers." Several executives view portions of the regulations with which their companies must comply as being impractical, unnecessary or, in a few instances, actually counterproductive to the improved safety of their products.

There are also complaints about "the nature of the regulators." "The major problem we face," one company's chief counsel relates, "is in the interface with governmental agencies. All too often, the agency people we work with are improperly trained and not as knowledgeable as they should be about the regulations they are enforcing." (See page 61.)

Another executive observes, "A lack of specific product knowledege and a heavy emphasis on enforcement of regulations, impedes the achievement of improved product-safety performance where it really counts—that is, in reducing injuries and fatalities. It is a costly, wasteful effort doomed to failure because it does not deal with motivating and educating workers and employees."

Too often, several executives say, their contacts with regulatory enforcement personnel reveal a lack of understanding about how products are manufactured and used. Another common complaint is concerned with the costs of complying with safety regulations. In a number of instances recordkeeping and reporting requirements are viewed as onerous.

Standards, Testing and Evaluation

Defining what is a "safe" product is seldom an easy or straightforward task. Companies seeking guidance from standards-setting organizations—either private or governmental—are often said to be getting incomplete or inconsistent help.

In the opinion of a number of safety executives, the testing procedures required for their companies' products are excessive and, in some cases, misdirected. For example, a food company executive asserts: "Governmental food regulations have had the effect of *increasing* the number of potentially unsafe contaminants. The problem is with legal adulteration, rather than with actual hazards.[1] Laboratory tests are becoming prohibitive on many products."

A similar complaint is voiced by another safety director, in the chemical industry, who says: "The Toxic Substances Act would divert resources from existing products, which legitimately need such attention, by reason of the fact that all new substances—harmful or not—would need clearance. The legislation leaves little room for sound, prudent judgment as to the applicability of testing and screening requirements."

Survey respondents would like to see industry test procedures standardized, and testing methods accepted by both state and federal regulators. They suggest also that more research effort be devoted to "hazard analysis"—an evaluation of the overall extent to which a new or existing product may constitute a real safety hazard when used or abused by consumers. Safety executives say that they recognize that the impetus for this kind of analysis must come from their own companies, rather than from regulators; but many believe that governmental agencies could assist company efforts by placing greater stress on the need for such analyses.

Altering Company Attitudes

As described elsewhere in this report, a major hurdle facing many safety executives is that of keeping safety issues in perspective for members of senior- and middle-management personnel. The problem is not so much one of convincing managers that company products should be

---

[1]The product may fail the legal criteria for safety acceptance (by reason of weight, color, ingredient content, etc.), yet represent no health hazard to the consumer.

safe—there is no disagreement with that thesis. Rather, the problem is one of apathy, unfamiliarity or misplaced priorities. One executive explains: "It is difficult to instill the concept that product safety is a positive function of the design, manufacture and sale of a consumer product. Managers are, of course, profit oriented and tend to give priorities to those functions with which they are most familiar—that is, production, quality assurance, design, and so on—even though they recognize the need for producing a safe product. Where product-safety activities are performed on an in-addition-to-other-duties basis they tend to receive a low priority, unless there is an active follow-up to be certain that the required work is done."

Another common situation is that existing in another firm where the manager finds "safety has never been a problem, so people do not think it necessary to devote an extraordinary amount of time to it." But this company's safety executive says that the future may hold some real safety risks for the firm.

A related concern is reported by a recreational products company spokesman who says: "Continuing problems develop among operating managers. We need the capability to make effective risk-benefit decisions as they relate to new and existing products, taking into account the future probability of escalating product-liability risks."

Some safety specialists see evidence that middle management has not yet begun to recognize fully the resources that are necessary to assure an effective product-safety program. One safety manager says: "The message finally gets across when the financial people see how product-liability insurance premiums are going up."

To achieve real success, however, there is said to be a need for a broad consensus that product-safety goals are essential and achievable. One safety professional talks in terms of obtaining a "totality" of involvement by all the company's operating divisions and their personnel. This manager sees the problem as being one of communication and hopes that improvements in this area will develop so that "problems or potential problems surface immediately and are passed along to the safety department."

The Product-Liability Impediment

There is little doubt, safety professionals say, that the time and expense required to investigate and assist in defending product-liability actions—either suits or complaints—does impinge on the time and budgets of safety units. Safety professionals recognize this as a necessary commitment, but at times agonize over the "costs" of such a commitment.

The safety manager in a chemicals company, for example, reports: "Many of our products are sold in relatively small orders, because of their special market applications, and we have some problems in monitoring all these claims and still providing more sophisticated testing programs for new products we might introduce. In addition, the time and effort required to defend product-liability suits of questionable merit, often on products many years old, detracts from more constructive product-safety efforts."

There are numerous reports of what safety professionals consider to be an "unreasonable number of complaints and claims," claims requesting excessive renumeration, and claims relating to products produced and sold long ago. (See box on page 10.) For such older products, it is sometimes difficult to effectively reduce the hazards associated with these products, particularly when, in some instances, the products have been modified by customers or are not actually separate and identifiable products, but are components of older systems that have since proved hazardous.

Several executives complain that such traditional allies as their insurance companies have not been helpful in assessing the liabilities that may exist for older products, and thus weighing the kinds of safety modifications that might be desirable—or the anticipated risks they may be facing from possible liability suits. Also, increasingly liberal damage awards are making it even more difficult to make such predictions.

Ironically, product complaints and lawsuits—and the climate that develops around such incidents—may actually inhibit certain companies from making products already sold more safe. Says one safety director: "Changing tort laws are such that product improvements could be used against us in some states. We have no way of putting on field units [i.e., machinery modifications to increase safety] because we don't know where the customers are, nor the impact that such improvements might have in the event of litigation. At the same time, we cannot force equipment owners to add safety equipment," nor can we afford to give it away".

At the same time, product-liability considerations force companies to be much more meticulous in maintaining safety records and test data. One aerospace producer says: "Our vulnerability to product-liability litigation requires that all product-safety efforts be carefully executed and recorded. Accident prevention must constantly be recognized as our number-one priority."

Some safety executives claim that constantly "looking over one's shoulder" for an impending lawsuit tends to have an inhibiting effect on product experimentation, innovative safety modifications, and so on. But many acknowledge, as well, that the threat of litigation has been one of the primary forces in getting their companies to take product safety more seriously than before.

Falling Behind Technology

More and more companies find that they must run faster just to stay even with the problems posed by safety-related issues involving product liability, regulatory requirements, and so on. Some find it very difficult. One executive explains: "Advancing technology is a nightmare for us. The technical capabilities of our products are advancing at such a rapid rate that the product-safety program is always at least one step behind. That is, our programs, tests, quality assurance, education, product use, and so on, cannot keep pace with the advancement in technology."

This situation can pose a personal dilemma for the safety professional attempting to keep abreast of the field. Furthermore, technological advances—particularly those applied to new products—can increase not only the products' complexity but also their potential hazards. A manager observes: "On a personal basis, you know that the more mechanical and electrical things you own, the more things there are to break down. For a manufacturer, the more parts, subsystems and systems we incorporate in a product, the more possibility that it also will break down—and some of these failures create safety hazards. The more complex products should not be more hazardous per se; but in practice it often seems to work out that way."

Similarly, product improvements may actually increase the time lag between when a company learns of a potential safety defect and its remedy. One safety executive gives, as an example, engineering changes made by his company, a producer of appliances, during the course of a particular model year's production. These changes—whose purposes are to improve product performance, lower manufacturing costs, and so forth—also introduce new variables into the manufacturing equation. Product failures—sometimes with safety consequences—may begin to take place in the field. At first, safety specialists may be perplexed as to how a product with an unblemished record has "suddenly become unsafe." The actual reason, the executive explains, may lie in the altered interrelationship between a large number of components that make up such a product. An in-process design change must be instituted only after a thorough evaluation of the impact the change may have on the safety balance of the finished product.

Solving Costs and Staffing Problems

The costs of measuring product hazards is said to be approaching almost prohibitive levels in some industries. Some managers wonder if their firms will be able to compete with others in their industry—in some instances with foreign producers as well—who, for a variety of reasons, may be less encumbered with safety standards. (For example, a recent survey of Japanese consumer products manufacturers found that up to four-fifths of the companies exporting products to the United States did not have product-liability insurance.)

Rising cost pressures are also a factor in staffing safety units. Several executives say that they are expected to accomplish expanded safety missions with little or no additions to staff. Even when budgets are increased, the company may experience some difficulty in finding technically qualified personnel.

The squeeze on safety budgets created by the necessity to meet regulations of CPSC, OHSA, and so forth, leaves some departments with little funds left for safety research and development. As a result, some safety professionals believe that they are forced to allocate funds to issues they consider to be of borderline or transitory value. Frustration is also reported over an inability to develop precise cost-benefit comparisons that might justify enlargements or reallocations of budgeted safety resources.

Organizational Shortcomings

Yet another obstacle to improved product-safety performance stems from the inadequacies of internal organization and procedure in some firms. Some units have yet to develop an effective means for getting wholehearted support for revised product instructions and adequate product standards.

In other instances, parallel reporting tracks—between product safety and quality assurance, for example—mean that, like railroad tracks, they disappear over the horizon without ever joining.

Safety efforts begun at a divisional level, in still other cases, have proliferated without sufficient corporate-level concern or coordination. For some, this has produced a duplication, and even a counterproductive approach to improving products' safety.

Trends in Product-Safety Programs

By a substantial majority, the safety executives surveyed by The Conference Board expect the pace of product-safety activities and programs in their companies to accelerate during the years immediately ahead. This prediction carries with it the belief that companies will need to devote more attention and resources to product safety and its related activities—such as quality assurance and consumer affairs. The principal reasons given for this forecast include the belief that there will be:

(1) A continuing proliferation of product-safety regulations.

(2) Additional increases in the volume of product-liability litigation.

(3) An increase in the attention management will be required to give to the financial impact of product-safety failures.

Some of those surveyed believe their firms may be increasingly affected by so-called single-issue product-safety statutes—for example, the Refrigerator Safety Act, the Poison Prevention Packaging Act, and the like. "The well is far from dry, as far as new safety laws are concerned," one safety manager says, "and legislators are aware that safety is a motherhood issue, one that fellow lawmakers will have a hard time voting against." At the same time, a number of consumer advocates are dissatisfied with the achievements of omnibus laws, such as the Consumer Product Safety Act and the Environmental Protection Act. These activists may seek more selectivity in product-safety regulations (thus increasing the total number of safety laws and regulations).

In several firms, according to the safety executives, the "costs of product safety" have only just begun to be tabulated. These firms have totaled the costs of increased product-liability insurance, the costs of recovering safety-defective products, the sums paid to dissatisfied customers, the amounts awarded by the courts to successful plaintiffs, and so forth—and have found the sum to be of "staggering proportions." Safety professionals say that such costs are almost certainly going to focus management's attention on safety activities in the years ahead.

However, a minority of the survey respondents—approximately one-third—believe that product-safety activities have most likely reached a plateau in their firms. The safety manager for one cosmetics firm says: "The product-safety issue isn't going to go away, and we're not about to disband our safety department, but we don't see any significant increase in either the number of complaints or suits filed against us. And our present staff can pretty well handle the regulations we're subject to."

And another safety executive, reflecting a similar view, notes: "The pace of product-safety activities is already pretty high. We don't anticipate any major increases. We think the regulators pretty much have their hands full trying to enforce safety laws that are already on the books, and we don't see any big new wave of safety legislation."

Observers in the legal community, however, feel that the pace of product-safety activities inside the average corporation will rise during the next decade. They reason that the external costs—primarily that of product-liability litigation and claims settlement—will put even greater pressure on companies to modify the safety practices of their employees. And it is at this juncture—that point where companies can influence the actions of their employees—that the focus of product-safety concern and activity will be centered. One legal commentator notes:

"Business operates through armies of employees, and it is indisputable that an employer can and does bring a pressure to bear upon his employees which has a greater effect upon them than would the remote chance of their being personally made defendants in suits. If actions were only permitted against employees, ordinarily they would not be brought. ('You can't get blood out of a stone—who ever sues the engineer of a negligently operated train?')[2]

Companies have begun to take a second look at employees' safety attitudes and practices. Sometimes they find that operating managers underestimate the company's liability and exposure, either disregarding or suppressing information on safety hazards that, if management were aware of, could probably be corrected. For example, one railroad had a highly hazardous crossing that company studies had shown could be safeguarded with an automatic crossing gate, a device that would probably reduce fatal accidents by 90 percent. Finally, after a 30-year- old truck driver had been killed at the railroad crossing, and the company was forced to pay $2 million in compensatory damages and $1.8 million in punitive damages, corrective action was taken. Two years after the trucker's death, the railroad installed automatic crossing gates to guard the crossing.[3]

In another instance, a steam vaporizer manufacturer reportedly received several complaints about scalding accidents—resulting from children accidentally tipping the vaporizer over. The company reportedly failed to heed these complaints, did not modify the product, and allegedly failed to take its insurance company's advice to recall its vaporizers. It was not until a three-year-old child was severely scalded with the product, and a jury awarded this child $150,000, that the company modified its product design and recalled the unsafe products.[4]

Product Safety's Impact on Other Company Activities

There are at least two corporate areas frequently mentioned as being likely to be substantially affected by future product-safety trends: new product development, and foreign operations.

In the opinion of several safety executives, what some members of industry have come to regard as "excessive" product-safety regulations may have reached the stage where they inhibit the development and introduction

[2]Thomas F. Lambert, Jr., "Suing for Safety," *Trial*, April, 1977, p. 45.

[3]Southern Pacific Transportation Company v. Lueck, 535 P. 22 399, 540 P. 12 1258 (Arizona 1975).

[4]McCormack v. Hankscraft Company, 154 N.W. II d 488 (Minnesota, 1967).

of new products. For example, it is pointed out that certain new product candidates are inevitably considered to be of "marginal" promise. If development and promotion costs can be kept within a certain budget, the limited market available to these products may still be large enough to guarantee a satisfactory return on investment. But some of the candidates are certain to fall by the wayside if development budgets have to be substantially expanded in order to provide for more rigorous product-testing requirements, as dictated by federal or state regulators—or even by a firm's own specialists.

Modifying the Product-Liability Environment

The Federal Government's Inter-Agency Task Force on Product Liability, in an interim briefing report, noted that product-liability litigation was increasing and was likely to continue to rise. But the Task Force did not see this as a universal phenomenon. It suggested, for example, that the "tort litigation system and the rise of product liability insurance premiums have been an effective spur towards inducing manufacturers to produce safe products....there is a school of economic thought that suggests that the current product liability insurance problem has placed too much of a burden on manufacturers to implement product liability prevention techniques. It is said that this is economically wasteful to force manufacturers to employ more product liability prevention techniques or devices than may be necessary in light of the fact that the user or consumer is sometimes the most 'efficient accident cause avoider'. This argument runs counter to today's strong social policy trend that seeks to protect the consumer in spite of his own carelessness."[1]

[1]*Briefing Report.* Inter-Agency Task Force on Product Liability, United States Department of Commerce, Jan. 1, 1977, p. 10.

The "swine flu" vaccine episode of several years ago may illustrate the point. In this case, companies were reluctant to produce the vaccine on a mass basis, being discouraged by the attendant liability and the unwillingness of insurers to underwrite the risk. Eventually, Congress stepped in and became the insurer of last resort. As it turned out, the vaccine did cause medical problems for a number of individuals, including some who contracted a paralyzing illness. As a result of the vaccine's use, liability suits for millions of dollars have been filed. And even though companies in such situations may be "protected" by federal statute, they must nevertheless defend themselves in court. The legal defense costs for such firms, or their insurers, may become so onerous that, in the future, they would be unwilling even to enter certain product areas—despite what legal shields might be erected for them.

However, a government study group that examined the impact of product-liability costs on new product development, reported: "We're not at all certain that the effect of product-liability suits on new product development has been *totally* [emphasis added] adverse. The system may have resulted in curtailing the production of unsafe products."[5]

Product Safety and the Export Market

Naturally, many U.S. manufacturers are worried over the impact of product-liability exposures they may face in foreign markets, especially in the Common Market Countries. Recently, the European Commission, the executive arm of the European Economic Community, developed guidelines intended to help standardize member nations' product-liability laws. These guides would create a strict code of product liability—a code to which U.S. producers shipping their products to European markets would be subject. Portions of the code state:

[5]*Briefing Report.* Op. cit.; p. 10.

text continued on page 118

Exhibit 41: Product-Liability Status in Europe and the United States

QUESTION	Who is liable—manufacturers, suppliers, or both?	Is privity of contract a requirement?	Does liability depend on a product defect?	Does liability depend on negligence?	On whom lies the burden of proof?	Are damages awarded for "pain and suffering?"	Are there limitations on damages?
BELGIUM	Either manufacturer or supplier may be liable.	No; contract provisions may preclude action in some cases.	Yes; but liability may in some cases be based on other causes.	Negligence is presumed if there is a defect.	On plaintiff to prove defect; on seller to prove defense.	Yes; indemnity may be for every type of injury, direct or indirect.	No limitations.
DENMARK	Any member of the supply chain may be liable.	Presence or absence of privity of contract has no effect.	No; the guiding concept is fault rather than defect.	Yes. Contributory negligence, assumption of risk, and negligence of 3rd party are defenses.	On plaintiff to prove damage; on defense to prove innocence of fault.	Yes. Also for medical expenses and loss of income.	No statutory limits. In practice, awards are limited by concept of average needs.
FRANCE	Either may be liable.	No; liability is based on fault.	Yes, in most cases. Vendors are presumed to know of defects.	No, but contributory negligence of plaintiff may reduce liability.	On plaintiff to prove tort; on seller to prove defense.	There is no specific rule; in general, all damages must be compensated.	No limit in principle. Awards based on extent of damages.
WEST GERMANY	Any member of the supply chain may be liable.	No; but privity of contract may offer some advantages to plaintiff.	Yes; included are defects in instructions for use.	Yes; element of negligence or fault must be present.	On plaintiff to prove damage and cause; on defense to prove innocence of fault.	Yes. Also expenses and loss of earnings.	No limit except extent of damages. Award may be reduced by contributory negligence.
ITALY	Either may be liable.	No; but privity may strengthen plaintiff's case.	Yes; defect must also have existed prior to sale.	Yes; negligence of 3rd party may reduce liability.	On plaintiff to prove defect and causation; on seller to prove defense.	Only for injuries resulting from a criminal offense. Expenses, loss of earnings compensated.	Awards generally determined by reference to tables or by concept of equitability.
THE NETHERLANDS	Either may be liable.	No; actions may be brought under either law of contract or tort.	Yes; included are defects in advertising or instructions.	Yes; contributory negligence may reduce liability.	On plaintiff to prove damage; on defense to prove innocence of fault.	Yes. Also for expenses and loss of earnings.	No statutory limits. Awards based on circumstances.
ENGLAND	Usually the manufacturer, occasionally the supplier.	No; but privity of contract may preclude action in tort.	No; manufacturer has duty to warn of dangers in use.	Yes; contributory or 3rd party negligence may reduce liability.	In general, on the plaintiff, but negligence may be inferred.	Yes. Also expenses and loss of earnings.	No statutory limits.
THE UNITED STATES	Anyone engaged in selling products may be liable.	Generally, no. The concept of privity has been retained in only a few states.	Yes, in most states. Seller must give proper warnings.	No; strict liability applies in most jurisdictions.	On plaintiff to prove defect and causation; on seller to prove his defense.	Yes. Also expenses and loss of earnings.	No limits, except under some wrongful death statutes.

Exhibit 41: Product-Liability Status in Europe and the United States (continued)

QUESTION	Is other compensation deducted?	If injuries are fatal, may heirs sue?	Are damages paid periodically or in lump sum?	Is insurance customary and available?	Are class action suits permitted?	Are contingency fees for attorneys permitted?	Who pays legal costs of plaintiff?
BELGIUM	No deduction for other insurance. Social security may be deducted, and may be subrogated.	Dependents, rather than heirs, may claim.	Lump sum.	Most manufacturers insure; suppliers with some exceptions usually do not.	No. Each plaintiff must act individually.	Percentage fees not permitted; but fees may be fixed on a scale according to importance of case.	Each party pays own fee. Court costs paid by unsuccessful party.
DENMARK	Not in product liability cases.	Yes; compensation may be inherited.	Lump sum.	Retailers insure under general liability policies; insurance for producers and wholesalers not widely used.	No. Danish law does not recognize class suits.	Contingency fees permissible, but subject to reduction by the court, and rare in practice.	Generally, the unsuccessful party must pay costs of both parties.
FRANCE	Social security is deducted; defendant must reimburse social security.	Yes; heirs may sue either on the victim's or their own account.	May be either.	Producers commonly insure; in some cases risk may be difficult to insure.	Associations may sue on behalf of groups; individual plaintiffs may not.	No. Contingency fees are illegal.	Plaintiff must pay his own attorney; damages may be increased to cover cost.
WEST GERMANY	Other insurance not deducted; insurer assumes victim's claim in most cases.	Yes; damages for pain and suffering must have been previously before the court.	Periodic payments. Lump sum may be paid under some circumstances.	Manufacturers nearly always covered under general liability policies; some specific product insurance used	Several plaintiffs may sue jointly, but one plaintiff may not sue for others.	No. Lawyers' fees are fixed by scale according to amount in dispute.	Successful party may claim court costs and lawyer's fees.
ITALY	No deduction for other insurance; social security may claim against defendant.	Yes; heirs may claim both for victim's damages and for loss of support.	Lump sum; usually; periodic payments in some circumstances.	Many manufacturers carry insurance; but practice is not general or customary.	Plaintiffs must sue individually, but cases may be joined.	No. Contingency fees are illegal; fees are set within a range according to work involved.	Plaintiff if successful may claim half his legal fees. Some costs awarded in full.
THE NETHERLANDS	Social security deducted. For other insurance, practice varies. Subrogation allowed.	Dependent family may sue in death from injuries; not in later death from other causes.	Lump sum usually; periodic payments in some cases.	Insurance is customary for manufacturers and large suppliers.	Class actions as such not recognized; plaintiffs may sue on behalf of other named parties.	No. Contingency fees not permitted.	Successful party usually awarded part of his legal costs.
ENGLAND	Social security may mitigate damages. Other insurance not deducted.	Yes. Heirs may claim victim's damages, dependents on their own account.	Lump sum.	Insurance is customary for both manufacturers and suppliers.	With exception of some fatal accident cases, one plaintiff may not sue on behalf of a group.	No. Contingency fees not permitted.	Successful party may claim all costs, in practice usually recovers about two-thirds.
THE UNITED STATES	In most jurisdictions, other compensation not deducted.	In common law, no; but statutes in many jurisdictions give cause of action.	Lump sum.	Insurance is commonly carried; suppliers may be protected by manufacturers.	Class actions permissible, but most courts slow to allow in personal injury cases.	Yes. Almost all personal injury cases handled on contingency fees from 1 3 to 1 2 of award.	No direct reimbursement for costs of either party; contingent fee paid out of award.

[1]Reprinted with permission of *The Journal of Insurance*, a publication of the Insurance Information Institute, New York, N.Y. The material originally appeared in the January/February 1977 issue, p. 26. The chart is based on papers published in *Product Liability in Europe*, edited by Paul M. Storm and distributed by Fred B. Rothman & Co., South Hackensack, N.J.

Another View of Product-Liability Reform

Not all observers view the current drive for reform of the strict liability in tort doctrine as beneficial to either the economy or society. Some critics worry that lawmakers will be panicked into permitting the erosion or removal of some of the basic protections now afforded consumers against defective products. These critics envision the entire tort reform movement as some kind of conspiracy to manipulate the legal system in such a manner as to roll the clock back to those days when consumers could sue successfully only when they could prove *deliberate* negligence on the part of producers.

This view of the tort liability reform movement, for example, is one that has been expressed by Ralph Nader, who had this to say: "The corporate assault on products liability is clearly an impending battle for the common law itself...there is now a tendency in corporate circles either to create an artificial shortage in order to get what corporations want—higher prices or less regulation—or to create a scare based on a wholly insupportable allegations. The latter is the case in the products liability struggle.

"The nature of the assaults on product liability is quite interesting. It is not just an attempt on [the part of] insurance and other companies to save themselves money: It is the dislike for decentralized decison-making in our legal system. The courts are the only decen-tralized forms for decision making in our legal system. There is only one Food and Drug Administration, one Congress. If you win, fine, but if you lose there is almost nowhere else to go.

"When you have thousands of federal and state courts all over the country, however, there is the greater probability of law being moved forward creatively, in some states initially further than in others...the products liability struggle is a clear manifestation of the political struggle that is going on between centralization and decentralization of power, and if trial lawyers do not start becoming aware of what's going on, they are going to be unable to make their cases as they must.

"The third reason for the attack on product liability is that insurers are very concerned about the discovery of information that they've held secret...I think it is very important to focus on the desire of these companies and the insurance industry to crack down on products liability in order to keep the flood gates from breaking open and spilling the information that could bring greater deterence, tougher safety standards, and more products liability lawsuits; and, of course, correction of the industrial processes causing the products defects in the first place."

[1]Ralph, Nader,"The Corporate Assault on Products Liability." *Trial,* October, 1977, p. 38.

Product Liability: Suggestions for Reform

A number of the safety professionals cooperating in this study view product-liability law as being in real need of reform. Among some of their suggestions, a majority of which would require revisions of state or federal legal codes, are these:

•The establishment of a product-liability statute of limitations based on the age of the product, rather than on the date that a consumer was injured by the product.

•Consideration of the state-of-the-art in product design as a defense in liability lawsuits. (At present, the fact that specific safety design features may not have been available at the time a product was manufactured is not an acceptable defense in many jurisdictions.)

•Consideration of the fact that a user's actions in modifying or materially changing the product, after it is purchased, may constitute contributory negligence when injury results from the subsequent use of the altered product. (It is suggested that negligence should be available to be cited as a defense against suits involving altered products—where such modifications have been deemed to produce a less safe product than the manufacturer originally sold.)

•A limitation on the percentage of an award that attorneys can receive under contingency-fee systems, in order to discourage so-called "ambulance chasing" by attorneys who may be inclined to prosecute less-than-legitimate product-liability cases. (Certain states have already adopted such limitations, or provided fee schedules that provide for reduced contingency-fee percentages in the case of major liability awards.)

•A limitation on liability for noneconomic loss—that is, loss incurred as a result of pain and suffering.

•A reform of the workers' compensation systems to compensate more adequately those injured in workplace accidents. Such a move, several executives say, would reduce the motivation for workers to sue suppliers of equipment and materials as a means of redressing what the workers perceive to be inadequate compensation as provided by workers' compensation statutes. (Recently, several states have begun to move in this direction.)

"Any person who imports into the European Community an article for resale or similar purchase shall be treated as its producer." Thus, U.S. firms' subsidiaries, or agents of U.S. firms, would be subject to the strict new product-liability code.

Further, the guidelines define a producer's liability in clear terms—terms that are, in the opinion of some observers, even more restrictive than the U.S. strict liability in tort statutes. Article I of the guidelines states:

"The producer of an article shall be liable for damage caused by defect in the article, whether or not he knew or could have known of the defect. The producer shall be liable even if the article could not have been regarded as defective in light of the scientific and technological developments at the time when he [it] put the article into circulation."

At present, practices and exposure risks involving product liability differ substantially among the countries that make up the European Economic Community. (See Exhibit 41.) Within France, Belgium and Luxemburg, product-liability case law is often similar to that of the United States—that is, charging the person (company) producing an article with strict liability, even where fault or negligence does not exist or cannot be proved.[6]

But in other European countries, a person claiming injury is required to prove negligence or fault on the part of the manufacturer. Thus, the burden of proof lies with the claimant; if unable to prove injury, the claimant must reimburse the defendant for all legal costs associated with the defense of the suit. (European consumer advocates have argued that this practice, and the absence of a contingency fee system, tends to discourage indigent and working-class claimants from prosecuting legitimate product-liability cases.)

Of course, the situation is not one-sided by any means, for foreign producers are known to be equally concerned about the doctrine of tort liability in the United States and the effect it is already having on their insurance rates. In this connection, the United States Department of Commerce has reported:

"Sharp product liability premium increases have not only affected American companies; we have received communications from the British Embassy that exporters in Great Britain have also experienced sharp premium increases with regards to goods destined for the United States."[7]

[6]"E.C. views greater liability for producers," *Report from Europe,* a survey by Chemical Bank, Vol. 3, No. 9, November, 1976. p.1.

[7]*Briefing Report.* Op. cit.; p. 8.